A CENTRAL AFRICAN ODYSSEY

A CENTRAL AFRICAN ODYSSEY

William W. Cowen, MBE

The Radcliffe Press
London · New York

Published in 1995 by
The Radcliffe Press
45 Bloomsbury Square
London WC1A 2HY

In the United States of America
and Canada distributed by
St Martin's Press
175 Fifth Avenue
New York
NY 10010

A full CIP record for this book is available from the British Library

Library of Congress Catalog card number: 95–067458

A full CIP record is available from the Library of Congress

ISBN 1–85043–923–0

Copy-edited and laser-set by Selro Publishing Services, Oxford
Printed and bound in Great Britain by WBC Ltd, Bridgend, Mid Glamorgan

Contents

Acronyms and Abbreviations

BBC	British Broadcasting Corporation
BOAC	British Overseas Airways Corporation
BSAP	British South Africa Police
C of E	Church of England
DDT	dichlorodiphenyltrichloroethane
MOH	Medical Officer of Health
NHS	National Health Service
PC	Police Constable
RAF	Royal Air Force
RF	Rhodesian Front
SRN	State Registered Nurse
UDI	Unilateral Declaration of Independence
UFP	United Federal Party
UNIP	United National Independence Party
VIP	Very Important Person
VSO	Voluntary Service Overseas
WNLA	Witwatersrand Native Labour Association
ZANU	Zimbabwe African Nationalist Union
ZAPU	Zimbabwe African People's Union

Glossary

Ag man!	Well!
biltong	strips of meat, dried and cured in the sun
boer	farmer
boma	fort
braaivleis	barbecue
bwana	Mr, master
dona	Mrs, madam
koppie	hill
kwatcha	national currency of Zambia
mabora	African name for Afrikaner, uncomplimentary
machila	sedan chair on a bicycle wheel
Munhu	African, man
munt	disrespectful term for black man derived from the Shona word, *munhu*
nganga	witch doctor
ngwee	national Zambian currency worth one hundredth of a *kwatcha*
nyoka	snake
promiso lo brocke	pull down your trousers
rooinek	redneck, pejorative term for Englishman
scop en msana	head and back
simbe	iron
sjambok	heavy whip of rhinoceros or hippopotamus hide
stukwan	elf
tackies	tennis shoes, plimsolls
Unshlungu	European

Acknowledgements

I wish to offer my thanks to Dr Lester Crook the publisher for his encouragement and help, Mrs Jill Edwards who miraculously managed to decipher my writing and typed the manuscript and to Mrs Selina Cohen of Selro Publishing Services in Oxford who expertly edited it.

Introduction

My main reason for writing this book is that it is a pleasant occupation to chronicle the memories of one's previous experiences as a means of consuming time during the long days of retirement. Another reason is the same as that given by Boccaccio, who is alleged to have explained after he had completed writing *The Decameron Nights* — 'it was in me and it had to come out!'

Practically all the books I have read about Central Africa (that part of Africa which, though not strictly in central Africa, was informally designated as such) — and there have been many — are works by journalists or government officials who have spent a limited time in Africa and they have researched deeply into political trends or given intellectual analyses of society there. My own treatise — which is completely unresearched — depends entirely on the memory of events as I personally experienced them, unless otherwise stated, before, during and after the federation of the British Central African territories. The chronological order of these events, depending entirely on memory, may possibly be wrong in detail and for this I beg forgiveness.

It was not my intention to write an autobiography but, of necessity, this became inevitable as I attempted to set down my own impressions and experiences during my youth and long working life spent in Africa, at the request of my son and his colleagues, who work in the discipline of economics in developing countries.

On their insistence special emphasis has been placed on race relations.

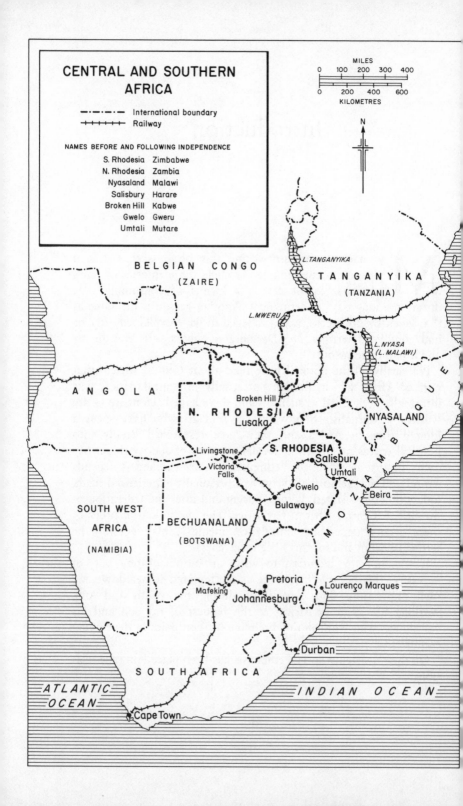

1

Prologue

Rural Essex can be seen rolling away through the window. This forgotten part of England is not the flat and uninteresting countryside associated with the better-known south industrial areas of the county. In the distance Suffolk sparkles in the sunlight and I am sure Cambridgeshire is visible on the horizon in the haze. This is glorious, lush English countryside rich in corn, barley and sugar-beet fields, only marred by the absence of hedgerows. In this age of mechanized farming, every inch of soil is valuable for crop production and an unimaginative government, or rather department of that government, has encouraged and subsidized the removal of hedgerows, with the result that the environment has deteriorated. Wildlife has suffered but the hedgerows, which mark the limits of this property, are intact and flourishing. A fine cock pheasant strolls across the lawn. Mallard ducks sit peacefully in close proximity to the pond. Moorhens are busy scratching around. Plover, wood pigeon, blackbird, sparrows, robins, tits and many other smaller birds abound. Life is uncomplicated and pleasant in this rural backwater. One is even able to visit village pubs where canned background music has not been installed. The locals are pleasant, happy individuals, still class conscious. The women, unaware of female lib, are happy to 'do' in the larger houses and the old pensioners are willing gardeners employed by the hour. The roads are not crowded and nobody appears to hurry. In short, life is very agreeable in the English countryside where the birds sing and the flowers are scented. For one who has experienced living there,

1

thoughts frequently envisage far off Africa. At times, one has an impulsive feeling to return to the so-called 'dark continent'. It is not only the sunshine and blue skies which are so appealing, but rather the whole concept of the environment of life in Central Africa — the vast wild countryside, the happy smiling indigenous population, the willing loyal servants, the outdoor pursuits and the free and easy attitude towards life in general. It is not difficult for those of us who experienced the good colonial life to understand why so many misguided Europeans were willing to fight and die for what they had cherished in central and southern Africa.

The relationship between an individual European and the indigenous African population in Central Africa will depend on the social, economic and educational background of the European concerned. As an illustration of what is meant by this statement, I had occasion to interview a recent immigrant to what was then Southern Rhodesia in the early 1960s.

He had served as a non-commissioned officer in the Royal Air Force in Rhodesia during the Second World War, and he informed me, in all seriousness, that he had left England and emigrated to Southern Rhodesia 'in order to get away from the blacks!'. He explained how the street where he lived, in his own property in Brighton, had deteriorated socially since his discharge from the forces and there were black families living nearby. He was well aware that under the unofficial apartheid system prevalent in Southern Rhodesia, whites and blacks did not mix socially. The blacks lived in their own suburbs completely separated from the white residents. They were only seen as servants who lived in rooms provided for them in the far end of European gardens.

In contradistinction to this incident, I knew of the case of the wife of an engine driver who had recently emigrated from the United Kingdom and was living in Livingstone. She considered it was her duty to wake her African servant each morning by taking a cup of coffee to him in his room in their garden.

She soon learned that this was not the usual practice and in order to conform with the prevailing race relations, she began to treat her black servants with disdain or, at best, with a paternalistic attitude. It is for this reason that I now set down, in some detail, my own background.

Prologue

My experience of central and South Africa was long and varied. I was born in Johannesburg, if not with a gold, then at least with a silver spoon in my mouth.· How far back one's memories of childhood events are reliable is debatable. Some will insist that even prenatal situations are remembered in later life. I certainly remember my preschool days from about the age of three years in a vague way. Odd events stand out clearly. There was a hill, or *koppie* in South African parlance, at the back of our house. From the top of this escarpment the central suburbs of Johannesburg rolled away to the horizon, scattered with glistening mine dumps. These dumps were the residue left after the ore, brought up from thousands of feet below the surface, had had the gold extracted. On a windy day clouds of white sandy dust would rise off the dumps. In the near distance trams could be seen travelling at regular intervals to the east. A short distance further on the main railway track — we lived to the north or right side of it — could clearly be seen wending its way in an easterly and southern direction. Local passenger trains stopped at two stations, while freight and main line trains went straight through. The comparatively high buildings of those days marked central or downtown Johannesburg in a southwesterly direction. The blacks lived in special townships or locations, far beyond the horizon in the same direction. This uninterrupted view, from the back of our house with moving trams and trains, left an indelible impression on my early childhood days and I have never lost my interest to this day in vehicles that run on rails. The hill I mention was part of a continuous range running through the gold-bearing reef and was known as the Witwatersrand or White Water Range.

I remember my European nurse taking me for walks over the hill and recollect that, on occasions, she met her lover and was kept busy while I was fascinated watching the trams and trains passing in the distance. It is odd how certain events stand out in dim childhood memories. At that time my parents and adults in general talked constantly about the First World War and speculated on who was winning, with emphasis on the conflicts in German East and West Africa.

I was sent to a small private preparatory school in the same road in which we lived. It was run by a kindly tall, thin, very English

3

lady, who was a strict disciplinarian and intent on making us proud to be part of the British Empire. Rule Britannia and God Save the King were sung daily. We had an end of term concert in which all the boys dressed up as sailors or soldiers and the girls as army nurses. More than 75 years later I recollect the first words of a song we were taught to sing — 'For it's the Navy, the British Navy that keeps our foes at bay' and it ended 'Britannia rules the waves, it never will be changed'. I have never lost my admiration and respect for the British tradition, which was thoroughly indoctrinated into us in those impressionable days of childhood.

I often search the recesses of my brain to try and recollect or visualize when I first became colour conscious. All the servants and unskilled workers were black, or in biblical terms, 'hewers of wood and drawers of water'. The black servants lived in outhouses in the gardens of European homes. They spoke their own language, ate different food and even to the very young child were obviously a different kind of human species. There was no social mixing between the races. They were referred to only by their Christian names and all black males, whatever their age, were called 'Boy'. It was inevitable that under the prevailing social structure the white child automatically became aware of his or her racial superiority. It was not unusual for white children to be young autocrats. Servants were instructed to do various tasks, which they were obliged to carry out without question. On one occasion my father, who was a big, jovial and kindly man, gave the 'house boy' a thrashing with a hose pipe because the servant had upset me in some way. I do not recollect the details but am sure I was responsible for the trouble. The 'boy' did not resist the thrashing in any way. At that time servants had to accept the authority of the master without question! I mention this episode because, with hindsight, certain events and experiences would influence thoughts and actions in later life. The basic injustice I observed on that occasion has never been forgotten and it is interesting that change has only come about recently — more than 70 years later. The new generation of blacks in Johannesburg is no longer willing to accept an abject state of servility. The recent riots in Johannesburg find their origin in longstanding, unacceptable human degradation. The challenge has been far longer in coming than I had anticipated.

The question of colour consciousness is not as simple as suggested. I am confident that young children are not colour conscious. The house next door to ours was occupied by a charming English lady and her three sons. The eldest son had joined the British South Africa Police in neighbouring Rhodesia. I was thrilled to hear about his adventurous life when he came home on leave, so that at an early age I was uncertain as to whether I would like to be an engine driver or a policeman. Their black female servant had a son living with her in the servants' quarters in their yard. He was about my own age and my joy in life was to play with him. Our main pastime was to drive hoops along the paths and pavements. I cannot remember whether I was duly reprimanded by my nurse or parents for playing with the little black boy next door, but most of our meetings were surreptitious as far I was concerned. Play felt lonely when he moved away with his mother.

The non-black population in Johannesburg was cosmopolitan. There was a constant stream of tradesmen and hawkers calling at the back of our home. The vegetable vendor or 'Sammy' was an Indian. In fact all Indian traders were referred to in this way. The laundryman, baker, iceman and many others selling chickens, eggs and so forth were usually Europeans. The most picturesque of these came around in ox wagons selling quinces, hard yellow peaches and other local fruits. These large ox wagons were drawn by about 14 oxen and were usually led by a young black. They carried enormous quantities of a particular fruit, covered with hay or straw, in the front part of the wagon. The back half of these sturdy vehicles with massive wheels were covered by a semicircular canvas dome. While the head of the family walked alongside the wagon with a large whip for the encouragement of the oxen, the female and younger members of the family were accommodated under the canvas awning at the rear of the wagon. The females wore bonnets. Whenever they came to a downward incline in the road, or wished to stop, the man with the whip would rush to the back of the wagon and hurriedly turn an iron handle, which would apply the large wooden brake blocks to the rear wheels.

My mother, in common with most other housewives at that time, was a keen home-preserving enthusiast. The pantry shelves were always full of glass bottles containing various fruits and jams.

The arrival of these fruit vendors was always a great occasion. Vast quantities of fruit were purchased at a ridiculously low price — as little as two shillings and sixpence or 30 new pence for 100 peaches was the usual asking price. We would stuff ourselves with these hard fruits before the boiling process commenced. This anecdote about the fruit sellers is recorded because it is one of my childhood memories that is significant. They were known to us as Boers — the Afrikaans word for farmers — and were also a race apart. They dressed and lived in a different manner from ourselves and spoke a different language. I was later to know them as Afrikaners or 'poor whites'.

It was now 1918. When the war ended I was seven years old. The armistice was a great occasion. People danced in the streets and all the tramcars were gaily decorated, such as they were on Empire Day or the King's Birthday.

Holidays were spent on my uncle's farm or at the seaside. An outstanding feature of these holidays was the train journey. On occasions stark naked African males were seen standing in the sidings where the train stopped. Unlike the fleeting, modern streaker, these naked gentlemen were not considered to be remarkable. It was all part of the passing scene. The most memorable holiday experienced as a child was a coastal trip from Durban to Cape Town. This was the first occasion I had left the shores of Africa and besides the thrill of a voyage on an ocean liner, the Royal Mail Steamer *Norman*, it was to initiate a lifelong interest in travel. The ship's crew, who were white Britishers, were quite unlike the colonial type of Englishman settled in South Africa. They came from a different social background. This was before the advent of Chinese, Lascar or other coloured crews. It was the first time I had seen Europeans performing manual labour.

Shortly before our return to Johannesburg from this trip, the 1922 white miners' revolution broke out. On our way home from the railway station we encountered a skirmish between mounted policemen and European workers from the gold mines who were on strike. Within a few weeks or days, the shooting part of the disorder commenced. I saw strikers shooting at an aeroplane from the hill at the back of our house. From the same vantage point troops could be seen disembarking from trains and actually being

6

shot at by strikers. A stray bullet went through the corrugated-iron roof of our servant's room in the back yard. It entered his thigh while he was sitting on his bed. Well do I remember the curfew, absence of transport, the food shortages and the disappearance of most blacks from the streets. This was an argument between whites and the blacks were not allowed to interfere. Once the strikers, who mostly came from the United Kingdom, had been completely routed and dealt with ruthlessly, life in the Golden City became normal once again and was comparatively pleasant for a young growing lad. It was not the overcrowded concrete jungle it is today.

My father, who was the pivot of my existence, frequently warned us about the 'Yellow Peril' we would encounter later in our lifetime. This referred to the Chinese, Japanese and other Asians. Significantly, at that time no one dreamed of the rise of the Afrikaners in South Africa or independent African states. Internationalism, in any form, was condemned, and the practice of Russian women going out to work while their children were educated in state crèches was considered to be unforgivable human degradation. In retrospect I was an immature young South African bourgeois, consciously and unconsciously aware of my racial superiority over the blacks, browns and non-English-speaking whites, proud to be part of the British Empire over which the sun never set. As a young South African I recognized four racial groups in the country — the large black indigent population, which did not seem to matter; the coloureds (mixed race), including the Indians and Chinese; the Boers or Afrikaners; and the group to which I belonged.

Between the ages of about ten to 12, Wednesday was a very important day because the English mail was delivered in Johannesburg weekly on that day. I impatiently awaited the arrival of the *Gem* and *Magnet* schoolboy magazines, which were published weekly. The *Magnet* written by Frank Richards and the *Gem* by Martin Clifford aroused my deep interest in the adventures of boys at English public schools. Not only were the characters of the outstanding boys at these schools, such as Harry Wharton and Billy Bunter at Greyfriars and Tom Merry at St Jim's, inspiring, but the stories in the *Gem* vividly described life in the nearby

English village. I remember all about PC Tozer who patrolled the area on his bicycle. These splendid authors of schoolboy adventures are mentioned because they inculcated in me a deep interest in England and its countryside. It made life at a South African school dull in comparison and it was at this comparatively early age that I decided I would prefer to live in England.

At the age of 13 I was sent to a famous South African school attached to the University of Cape Town. Cape Town is nearly 1000 miles from Johannesburg and is at sea level, i.e. 6000 feet lower in altitude than Johannesburg. It was said that Cape Town, the Garden City, was a similar amount lower in animation and smartness than Johannesburg, the Golden City. I would agree that this was a fair, accurate description, but what it lacked in liveliness it made up for in culture.

The school was situated in an extremely pleasant part of the old town between the city centre and the foot of Table Mountain. A comparatively small number of pupils were boarders and we naturally felt very superior. We would boast that a disproportionately large number of boarders were to be found in the various sports teams and extramural activities. The dayboys were considered to be inadequate. One soon became used to the regimented routine of existence in boarding school. To have cold showers at six every morning, come sun or snow on the mountain, was a ritual of honour and woe betide any boy who attempted to evade this masochistic habit. He would soon be dealt with by his peers. The masters, who were practically all Englishmen, were outstanding characters who commanded rather than asked for respect. We were treated as young adults and given a large degree of freedom. The school was for European boys only. We studied world history in general and South African history in particular. Except for mention of certain 'Kaffir Wars' and Bushmen and Hottentot tribes, who were the original inhabitants in the Cape Town area, in their historical context, no mention was ever made of race relations as a contemporary problem. Incidentally, the word 'Kaffir', which is the Arabic word for non-believer, was used as a pejorative term for any black person in Africa.

On Saturdays we played inter-school rugby or cricket, depending on the season, and visited nearby towns such as Paarl or Stellenbosch. I have fond recollections of the beautiful old town of Stellenbosch, with its oak-lined streets and open, clear streams running alongside the pavements. On Saturday nights, unless occupied in some school activity, we were allowed to go to the cinema. The films were silent and the cinema orchestra was appreciated more than the films. Cape Town was a beautiful old city with a very fine oak-lined avenue and gardens leading from our schoolhouse to the town centre and the main street had one side reserved for flower sellers. The massed flowers were a picturesque sight to find in a busy city centre. The flower sellers, who were all coloured, spoke Afrikaans which was their mother tongue. The majority of servants and manual workers in Cape Town at that time were coloured or of mixed race. Blacks were few and far between. On weekends we were allowed to go swimming or surfing in the summer months and walked many miles along beautiful scenic marine paths and roads, or climbed Table Mountain. Another Sunday afternoon attraction was to attend concerts by the Cape Town Symphony Orchestra, which performed on the old pier at the bottom of Adderley Street, the main street in the city. A fine open electric tramcar curled its way over the lower slopes of Table Mountain. Unfortunately, the price of progress has been the disappearance of these facilities. The sea has been reclaimed around the old pier, which is now part of the dock area. The mountain tramway has been replaced by motorways.

My favourite pastime was to go down to the docks on Sundays, which were out of bounds, most likely because of some undue influence ships and sailors may have had on schoolboys! The docks were deserted and quiet on Sundays as no loading and unloading of ships was allowed on the day of rest. Most of the big liners and freighters would leave port by Saturday and the weekly mail ship from England would arrive in Table Bay early on Monday morning. On occasion I was allowed to see relatives or friends off on the mail boat, which left for England at 4.00 p.m. every Friday afternoon. This was quite an event and thrill in Cape Town. The special boat trains, one from Johannesburg and the other from Rhodesia, arrived at the docks a couple of hours before sailing time. Hundreds of passengers, friends and onlookers milled around the quay and those with passes, which were easy to obtain, were allowed on the ship. The band played and it was always a sombre experience as the liner pulled away from the quay to the strains of Auld Lang Syne and God Save the King. Streamers were thrown and mail was hoisted onto the ship until the last moment of sailing. These were the days before intercontinental air travel.

One sunny afternoon I was strolling round the quays absorbed by the cargo ships in dock, noting their nationality and ports of origin from the four corners of the world — ports of registration of convenience, such as Liberia and Panama, had not been thought of — when I came upon a chance happening, which was to be a milestone in my life. I stopped alongside an American freighter. In the well deck a sailor was taking a snapshot of a colleague. What was so remarkable was the fact that the sailor taking the photograph was a black man. Although he had an American accent, he conversed perfectly in English. This was my very first experience of an obviously educated black man actually handling a camera. In my youthful ignorance it had not occurred to me before that this was possible either at present or in the future. I lay awake that night thinking and wondering about the phenomenon and have frequently recalled the episode. Perhaps my attitude to this happening was a personal idiosyncrasy because when I related my experience to fellow pupils their attitude was one of disinterest and I would venture to suggest that this was the position with regard to race relations at the time. There was an absence of interest.

The majority of coloureds or mixed race in Cape Town lived in a slum area in the city known as District Six. The blacks lived in townships or locations outside the city limits. I had never visited these areas and my first contact with District Six was rather unexpected. A classmate and fellow border persuaded me to forego a Saturday night cinema and suggested we went on the town and had fun. I yielded to the temptation. After visiting a pub, where we had beer shandies, we walked along the Marine Drive with the railway marshalling yards on one side and the sea on the other. Some distance along the drive we came to an overhead pedestrian crossing over the railway tracks leading to District Six. While walking along the overhead bridge a young coloured girl came in the opposite direction. My friend accosted her and, following a short introductory hug, I was horrified to see her being raped, if that can be the right word, because her protestations were perfunctory. Following this little episode we carried on into District Six and went into one of the sleazy drinking establishments. I was petrified to be in this area where no other white folk were evident and was pleased to leave. This was the first time I had witnessed any form of contact between the races in South Africa.

This was the beginning of the era of Afrikaans nationalism in South Africa. In Cape Town more individuals, including Europeans and coloureds, spoke Afrikaans rather than English and Afrikaans was a subject that could be taken at school. For myself, and those of similar tradition, it was the fashion not to familiarize oneself with this unpleasant sounding jargon. Was it not the language of the Boers and coloureds? In certain quarters opposition to non-Afrikaans-speaking individuals was becoming evident.

One Sunday I was allowed to visit the home of a day scholar classmate who lived in an outer suburb of Cape Town. In the evening, on my way back to school by bus, we passed nearby District Six and suddenly came upon numerous policemen with batons charging rioting coloureds. Stones were thrown at the bus, which kept moving along the road at a fast speed. Windows were shattered by the stones and, following the example of other passengers, I spent the next part of the journey lying on the seat in order to prevent my head being a sitting target. The newspaper the next day fully reported the riots, which were in opposition to the introduction of a new national flag in South Africa. As far as I can remember, the coloured community and others objected to the government's intention to abolish the Union Jack and that the new flag did not display the Union Jack as a major part of its design.

Summer and Christmas holidays were spent in Johannesburg. The train trip to and from home was an outstanding pleasure. The excitement of departure and arrival, the comfortable sleeping arrangements — the journey took two nights and nearly two days by fast express — the good food and service, the pleasant soothing click of wheels over joints, the chuffing of the powerful steam engines, the impressive scenery climbing up or down the steep Hex River Mountains and happy evenings spent in the dining car with other scholars of both sexes all bring back happy memories. The train crews, such as conductors, stewards and guards were, for the main part, English-speaking South Africans or Englishmen. Scullions and bed makers were of mixed race. At this time the authorities decided to electrify the railway system or parts of it throughout the country. A short passenger line in Cape Town, which ran from Adderley Street near the old pier for about two or three miles along the coast to Sea Point, a pleasant suburb of the city where we frequently bathed, was the first to be electrified and used as a training section for staff. My curiosity was aroused by the sight of a railway train without an engine and I joined the interested onlookers watching the trial trains coming into Sea Point station. The usual questions were asked about the new form of transport and a driver volunteered the information that he was training the 'local baboons' to work the thing but that they would eventually take over and he would lose his job. He was an Englishman referring to Afrikaans European railway workers.

I was now aged about 16 and due to matriculate. In retrospect, I did not find my schooldays unpleasant and I am pleased that I attended boarding school. It tended to make one more independent in outlook and inculcated a sense of discipline and loyalty. When I departed from school for the last time I had personally experienced public violence on two occasions and, in an unsophisticated way, was aware that race relations between black and white, coloured and white and white and white were not exactly Elysian in South Africa. Frequent visits to Cape Town docks had inculcated a desire to travel and see the world. Given the choice, I would rather have set sail on the 4.00 p.m. mail boat for England in preference to boarding the 4.00 p.m. mail train to Johannesburg.

* * *

My family were keen that I should take up a profession upon matriculation, but with the impetuosity of youth I flatly rejected the offer and as a compromise joined the family business and became a part-time student at the University of Witwatersrand, where I attended lectures in the faculty of commerce in the early mornings and evenings. It soon became evident to me that this way of life was unsuitable. As far as I was concerned commerce was not merely a matter of buying and selling. It was mostly scheming with a modicum of organization. We imported and sold farmers' equipment such as incubators and cream separators. It was the golden age of capitalism, and competition was rife. Some goods were sold at an exorbitant profit and others at a loss depending on the degree of competition. Employees worked extremely hard for long hours. I cannot surmise what motivated their loyalty and earnestness but this was an era when pride in one's work was very important. Remuneration was not nearly as important as it is today. Another example of competition was found in the pubs where, for the price of a beer, so many free snacks were offered that it was not necessary to order a meal.

I was allowed to join a university students' tour of England and the continent of Europe. My ambition to sail out of Table Bay had at last materialized. We were a small congenial crowd of students from various South African universities and were looked after by local student organizations in whichever country we visited. We toured practically the whole of Western Europe and mostly lived in university quarters during their Christmas vacation. My first experience of European culture was edifying. Theatres, art galleries and ancient universities were cognizant of past human achievements not available in South Africa. Germany was the only country where we had difficulty. We were admonished by the police on two occasions, one for singing in the street at night and the other for pushing a couple of female students on a porter's trolley at the Munich museum. The Germans seemed to lack any sense of humour, reflected in the students who took life very seriously and consumed vast quantities of beer. It was incumbent upon us to emulate their drinking capacity. A large number of their male students had scarred faces as a result of their practice of duelling.

Two female students and myself were arranging our sea trip back from Holland to England when it was suggested that we should rather fly. KLM had recently inaugurated a daily flight from Amsterdam to Croydon in London. As students we were offered a chance to fly at a ridiculously low fare — much less than the sea crossing. It was the first time any of us had been in the air and the trip in a Fokker aircraft was more exciting than anticipated. The aircraft, which could accommodate about a dozen passengers, with the exception of four seats, had had all the others removed and was loaded with cardboard boxes of tulips. We were the only passengers. The two crew members had on great leather coats with head coverings of the same material and goggles. We found the passage very bumpy and cold and my two female companions spent most of the time being airsick. The complete tour lasted three months including the sea voyages, which took 17 days by fast mail steamer to travel from Cape Town to Southampton and vice versa. A short while after my return to Johannesburg my mother died. I was very unsettled and decided to leave South Africa for good and once again sailed for England.

* * *

On arrival in London I shared digs with an old school friend who was studying medicine at a London hospital. I had little idea of what I intended doing for a living, but had decided to approach one of the manufacturers who supplied our firm in South Africa for employment. On my first Saturday in London I was requested to play as a substitute in a hospital rugby team where my friend was a student. The next week I had lunch with him in the students' restaurant. The whole atmosphere, attitude and character of student life, as I experienced it, appealed to me to such an extent that I applied to the dean of the medical college and was accepted as a student. As I had matriculated, the only other qualification required seemed to be the fact that I played rugby.

My life as a student for the next five years was arduous. I worked hard because I did not have a rich parent paying my study fees and upkeep. Life in digs was cramped, uncomfortable and at times lonely. London was far more pleasant than it is today. Living there gave one a sense of being at the centre of the world. There was a pervading impression of history and antiquity to be found in its streets and buildings. A walk through present-day London may be a more salubrious experience, but the old grime-encrusted buildings in a gloomy murky atmosphere had more fascination for someone used to the bright African sunshine than the many new clean, characterless buildings and houses in modern London.

There are many happy memories of student life. Frequent visits to theatres and cinemas and the Brasserie public house in Piccadilly, or 'Brasses' as it was popularly known, after rugby on Saturdays in winter, was always pleasurable with its beer-swilling students and happy, gay and unwholesome atmosphere. It was difficult to be bored in London. Even a stroll through the West End, mingling with the theatre crowds by night or the expensive looking shoppers in Regent or Bond Street by day was an interesting experience. As Commonwealth students we were well looked after by various institutions such as the Victoria League. We were invited to dances, concerts and had frequent invitations to spend the day or weekends with families in the countryside. The opportunity to experience life in the English countryside confirmed my desire to live there some day.

My income came from South Africa and exchange rates were in our favour following devaluation of the pound to such an extent that I was comparatively well off as a student and put into the middle or upper-middle-class income group. Class distinction was very evident in England. The newspaper vendors respectfully murmured 'thank you, sir' for my halfpenny, while a gentleman with a muffler instead of a tie, or cap in preference to a bowler usually had a 'watcha mate' response for his money. Male and female servants were obsequious and we were always referred to as 'young sir' by porters and others who considered themselves part of a lower strata. The middle and upper classes took advantage of the severe economic depression of the time. I employed a part-time servant or 'skivvy', as they were known, to do my washing, darning and prepare occasional evening meals. Their pay was never more than a £1.00 a week and there were many willing applicants for the job. Waiters and other menials were often made to feel servile by the condescending attitude of their betters. For this reason British Ocean liners were reputedly more popular, even among foreigners, because it was accepted that the stewards knew how to serve. On some ocean trips I did have the experience of being served by several 'gentlemen's gentlemen' — to use a proud description of themselves.

Depending on the individual, student life could be very irresponsible. By far the greater majority of my fellow students had done the first three years of their course at Oxford or Cambridge and were condescending to those of us who had not attended one of these two famous universities. In turn, we thought these types immature compared with the large number of empire colonial students in London.

Unlike the present time, one was allowed to have as many attempts at the final examination as one wished. I, personally, knew three students, two of whom were South Africans, who had been medical students in London for over 12 years. As long as their parents were willing to pay, they carried on enjoying their carefree, irresponsible existence. Contrary to what may be expected, they made excellent professional men when they did eventually qualify.

Student grants were unknown and academic achievement seemed to be less important than appearance, background and sporting prowess in the selection of students. A very small number worked their way through university. One of my colleagues worked as a barber in the evenings and weekends in order to support himself, and another worked on a night shift in a bakery, but this was unusual.

We often got up to all sorts of frivolous pranks. On one occasion, while travelling home on a crowded District Line train, I took my packet of cigarettes out of my pocket and, on pushing it open, four human fingers popped into view where cigarettes should have been. Fortunately I was quickly able to close the packet before it was seen by any other traveller. Womanizing, gambling and pub crawling were the popular vices of the day. The dean of our college, who was an understanding dear old academician, spent a great deal of his time sorting out the human problems of students. In one instance an elephant complicated the human interest. A student who lived near Tilbury told us of how he frequented a public house near the docks and, one night, at the end of a long session he jokingly agreed to buy an elephant at the docks for one shilling from one of the gentlemen drinking with him, and he signed an agreement for the purchase of the elephant at the offered price. To cut a long story short, there was a glut of elephants on the market and the next day our student friend was requested to arrange for the upkeep and feeding of the elephant, which was now legally his property. The beast was eventually

16

accepted by a zoo in the Midlands on the understanding that they did not have to pay for it. It cost his father a large sum of money to arrange for its transportation to the zoo.

Having completed our basic science subjects, anatomy and physiology, we graduated into the hospital wards and worked under chiefs or consultants who were physicians and surgeons in charge of patients. Some were in charge of specialist departments such as gynaecology or ophthalmology. The word 'chief' was an appropriate name for these autocrats who built up an aura around themselves and were accepted by others as very important individuals. These were the days before the National Health Service and the chiefs worked on an unpaid basis in the voluntary hospitals where we trained. They had private consulting rooms in or near Harley Street where they saw private patients. They maintained a dignified appearance and wore a uniform consisting of black frock coat or black jacket and striped trousers. White, stiff winged collars with silver tie or cravat were obligatory. Headgear consisted of a top hat or bowler later replaced by the 'Anthony Eden' large black felt hat. When they appeared at the hospital for a ward round or operating session they were met in the foyer by their registrar or first assistant, houseman and four students (which made up a firm) as they stepped out of their chauffeur-driven Rolls-Royce. The less famous, or less wealthy, who drove their own cars, were met at the ward entrance in a similar manner. It was incumbent upon the ward sister and her nursing staff on duty to meet the chief, standing respectfully to attention. Long sleeves and hard wrist cuffs were suitably worn for the occasion. The attitude of the chiefs to their students was ambivalent. Respect was overtly mutual and we were not treated as the young fiends we obviously were. After all, the supply of their future private patients depended on our goodwill. These gentlemen who were to teach us our skills and attitudes to our profession were a mixed bag. Some were good and others were bad teachers. Some were skilled and, rather surprisingly, others poor surgical operators. All were sure of their own importance. It was disappointing to discover some of these prominent individuals cheating. I observed a chief examining the X-ray plate of a patient in the radiological department and, a short while later on a ward round he brilliantly diagnosed the case under the pretence that he had not previously seen the X-ray. The impecunious pathologists and other full-time more scientific professors and lecturers were our real learned mentors. In retrospect, we had an excellent training in the art and practical skills of medical practice. Throughout the training, emphasis was placed on the ethics of our future profession. Very few diseases were amenable to treatment. The chemistry of the body, with its electrolytes and enzymes, had not been researched to any useful extent when compared with the position today. Anaesthetics were crude and antibiotics had not been discovered.

Each year I visited some part of the European continent, including places as far away as Russia or the Middle East. At Christmas we went on skiing trips to Switzerland. I had been a student for about four years and did not miss Africa in any way that I can recollect. In fact I told my colleagues that I did not ever want to return there. In a particularly bad winter, with almost constant fogs, some of pea soup intensity, when at times it never became light at all during the so-called daylight hours, a travel agent at the bottom of the Haymarket displayed a large artificially sunlit view of Table Bay and Cape Town. It looked very realistic and made one nostalgic. The continual dreadful weather was depressing and one day I impulsively went into the travel agent's establishment and booked my passage to South Africa. Travel charges were extremely cheap for students. The return fare by mail boat, tourist class, was £30. I thoroughly enjoyed the break in the sunshine and, on my return, realized that I was an African and would return there one day willy-nilly.

The study of medicine became more interesting as time passed and one became attached to the various specialist departments. There was a strong inclination to specialize in the subject you happened to be taking at the time. The mass of knowledge gained began to fall in place like a completed jigsaw puzzle. A worrying aspect of being a medical student was the fact that, until such time as you qualified, your competence to earn a living was just about nil, whereas the day your successful final results were published your courtesy title opened up the prospect of perpetual respect and wealth. The inevitable result was that most conscientious students became almost neurotic in their impatient desire to qualify and some, including myself, tended to overwork during the period leading up to examinations.

This was the epoch of political crisis and change. The king had died and the new king had abdicated. Nazism was established in Germany and Fascism in Italy. Chamberlain had accepted Hitler's guarantee of peace and I was in a West End cinema one evening when the news film showed Chamberlain's arrival by air from Berchtesgaden, where he had seen Hitler, and he waved a signed piece of paper, which was the alleged guarantee of peace. There was spontaneous booing from the audience. Mosley's British Union of Fascists was active, especially in Brighton and the East End of London and the Spanish Civil War was being fought out. There was very little political activity among the students and staff and I do not recollect being aware of any overt hostility to Nazism. Politics, international or national, was rarely discussed.

As stated, the medical course was long and arduous, but the five and a half years eventually passed and, one winter's evening, I hazily recollect taking a very shortened version of the Hippocratic oath and felt enchanted at the prospect of halcyon days ahead.

Unlike the present time it was not incumbent upon a recently qualified medical practitioner to work as a houseman or junior resident doctor in a hospital. He was licensed to practise all branches of medicine and surgery on qualification, but most of us did a varying number of six-month stints as houseman or junior resident doctor in a hospital before deciding on a permanent career in any particular branch of the profession. In these prewar years, it was now 1937, society had not become acquisitive or downright greedy. It was not easy for a colonial to understand how little the average citizen in the United Kingdom wanted to escape from his or her drab existence. The welfare state had not arrived, nor was it impending. Wages were low and unemployment high.

I worked in various hospitals in and around London. They were all voluntary hospitals, which meant they were supported by voluntary subscriptions, a euphemism for charity, and were self-governing institutions. One of my first jobs was as casualty officer at a well-known London hospital in the Strand. I could hardly have been in a more exciting precinct. Emergencies were brought into casualty day and night as the result of accidents, assaults, or severely ill individuals who had collapsed from a variety of causes. Our patients were visitors from all over the world, hotel workers, those connected with the entertainment industry, tramps or even prostitutes. During the first week there I was severely censured by a surgical consultant for sending two cases of fractured femur to his ward one day. These cases would 'block his beds and not be useful for teaching purposes'. The next unfortunate individual with a fractured femur had to undergo the pain and inconvenience of being refused admission from the casualty department and was transferred to a council or public hospital, which were obliged, by law, to admit all patients requiring hospitalization. The advent of the National Health Service, which put all hospitals under state control, did away with this iniquitous state of affairs.

Junior house doctors were unpaid or paid very little, but accommodation, food, laundry and beer were all provided free. This led to some bizarre consequences. We earned our cash income, for what it was worth, by performing medico-legal post-mortems in cases of sudden death, or appearing in court as an expert witness if an injured party, in its literal sense, considered litigation necessary in order to obtain fair compensation. In one case the houseman involved was so enthusiastic that he inadvertently agreed to appear on behalf of both the prosecution and defence in the same case. When it came to court the judge was understandably very derogatory in his remarks about the medical expert, who was duly reprimanded for his irresponsibility and warned about the possibility of being guilty of perjury. The judge ruled that the medical evidence be dispensed with in that particular case.

Only when I went to work as a house physician in Grimsby did I realize how dreadful life could be for some less fortunate individuals. Grimsby was designated a depressed area, in other words an area in which 50 per cent of the working population was unemployed. The majority of workers were fishermen who led a tough existence going out in deep-sea trawlers for weeks at a time. They fished in northern waters as far off as the Murmansk coast. As often as not the weather was foul, the sea rough and, on occasions, the crew were not dry for the entire voyage.

We had the unique experience of seeing the end results of disease because so many of our patients had become sick while at sea and adequate diagnosis and treatment only became available when they returned to port. As mentioned previously, the treatment of most prevalent diseases was unsatisfactory. Bed rest, good nursing and a bland diet — whatever that may mean — were the accepted treatment of many ailments such as pneumonia and tuberculosis. I had now had enough experience to realize where my interest in the practice of medicine was directed. Surgery I found too mechanical and the average surgeon, like the Thespians of old, often became melodramatic individuals, demanding and discourteous to those working under them. There was, however, one branch of medicine in which I believed the diagnosis of disease was in the main scientific and definite and treatment was also satisfactory. This was in the sphere of diseases peculiar to the tropics. I had made up my mind to specialize in tropical diseases and applied for and was appointed as house physician to the Hospital for Tropical Diseases in London.

While working at Grimsby it would have been difficult for an individual with even a modicum of interest in his fellow beings not to become interested in, and have some reservations about, the political and economic systems that controlled the destinies of men and events.

Although working in a designated distressed area, many of our patients in hospital were Icelandic or German fishermen. If more than 50 per cent of our own fishermen were unemployed, why were foreign ships landing fish in Grimsby? The explanation to my query came from an unexpected source. At a party in London one weekend I met a senior official in the Department of Agriculture and Fisheries who explained that the coal miners' lobby had more influence in the House of Commons than that of the trawler owners — hence the dumping of British coal in Iceland and the reciprocal dumping of fish in England. Another point of interest was that Grimsby, a distressed area, returned a Tory MP to parliament. The explanation I was given, for what it was worth, was that certain public houses in the town served cheap beer subsidized by the Conservative Party and paid the barman to spread Tory propaganda.

I later did a short locum for a poor-law doctor in the town and saw incredible poverty and human degradation, especially among the aged. Malnutrition was common in the young and the old. Many seemed to have lost interest in their very existence. I attended old people living in hovels, in some cases in a loft where the sun never shone. I often thought that primitive Africans who lived in mud huts in an African village that had not yet reached the stage of a cash economy were, by comparison, far better off. At least they had the advantage of being able to lie in the sun.

Life at the Hospital for Tropical Diseases in London was completely different. A large part of the flourishing British Empire was in tropical areas and, in addition to the many colonial civil servants, business executives and others employed by British firms in tropical areas, were our patients. These were middle or upper-middle-class individuals, usually accommodated in private wards, who at times would be very demanding. They presented a variety of tropical diseases, which were invariably diagnosed in the laboratory by a microscopic examination of blood smears or excreta. The senior resident at the hospital was interested in tropical medicine for the same reason as myself. He had never been abroad, but was so disillusioned by the attitude of the patients that he decided not to go to a tropical country and became a radiologist in England instead.

There was a premature war scare while I was resident at the Hospital for Tropical Diseases. All patients were discharged, the basement of the hospital was converted into an emergency operating theatre and large supplies of dressings, splints and other equipment suitable for the treatment of war casualties were brought in. Quantities of sand were dumped on the pavement outside the hospital. We sat and waited for about a week, eagerly reading the papers, listening to the wireless and awaiting the first bomb to fall with pleasurable anticipation and excitement. Fortunately it never materialized.

Following the usual six-month appointment at the hospital, I attended a course of study for a diploma in tropical medicine and hygiene at the Institute of Tropical Medicine and Hygiene. The course lasted an academic year and was of absorbing interest. On successfully completing my examination I decided to have another short holiday in Africa and to read for my membership, or higher general medicine diploma, on my return. I sailed in the old *Windsor Castle* and, as there were very few passengers, I spent most of my time with the ship's officers. It was one of the most pleasant of the many voyages I had experienced between the United Kingdom and Cape Town. We often discussed what would happen if war were to be declared while we were at sea. The captain was of the opinion that we could forget about the war, especially because of false scares during the past few years. On the liner's return trip from South Africa to England, as I was to discover some years later, she was torpedoed and sank with the loss of all hands on board.

I found South Africa totally different from the place I had known in my childhood. The English influence had gone and it seemed America was now the main inspiration, especially in the towns with their high rectangular buildings, glaring advertising hoardings and scurrying people. The Afrikaner had now come into his own and there were few English-speaking civil servants. The ox wagon was a thing of the past. I was spending a holiday with a married sister in Johannesburg. On the first Sunday in September we were playing tennis when she came out and told us that war had been declared, according to a statement over the radio by Prime Minister Chamberlain. I clearly remember that, in the glorious sunshine 6000 miles away from it all, we finished our set before coming in to consider the momentous news. The next day I tried to arrange my passage back to England, but all bookings had been cancelled. It was not at all definite that South Africa would join the war and, in fact, it did take another four days before Smuts, the prime minister, was able to overcome the opposition and declare war as an ally of the United Kingdom. In the meantime I had cabled the director of medical services in Rhodesia offering my services for recruitment in the armed forces. I received a cable of acceptance and left Johannesburg for Bulawayo on the last train before the border was temporarily closed, the day after war was declared.

2

Southern Rhodesia and Kenya

S outhern Rhodesia, which adjoins South Africa on its
northern border, is a vast land-locked territory. I had always
considered it to be British territory and remembered the
result of a referendum by Rhodesians in 1923 on whether they
should join up with the Union of South Africa or remain independent. They chose the latter.

The country was named after Cecil Rhodes — a great British
patriot — who was instrumental in conquering the territory from
the blacks for Britain at the turn of the century. Without having
visited Rhodesia, I cherished an inherent feeling of cordiality
towards the country and its people because of what it represented
when compared to South Africa. It was a relatively underdeveloped country and I regarded my projected arrival there with a
sense of adventure.

The railway line from Johannesburg to Bulawayo is anything but
direct from a geographical aspect. It passes along the Witwatersrand in a westerly direction, winds and climbs through the fertile
Magaliesberg Valley and then through the prairie-like Highveld —
one of the richest maize-growing areas in Africa. It then passes
from this rich arable area into equally rich pastoral bush country
where sleek cattle thrive. On arrival at Mafeking it joins up with
the main line from Cape Town and turns northward through
Botswana, which was then known as Bechuanaland. After another
24 hours and 580 miles further on Bulawayo is eventually reached.
This was alleged to be the longest through run in the world for a
steam engine. The track passes through flat bush country near the

24

Kalahari Desert. It was a hot and dusty journey. About half way an extended stop was made at Mahalapi, a small railway station where the engine had attention to its boiler and its tender re-coaled. The water tanks of the carriages were refilled, the local railway workers bought fresh fish and other perishable foods from the dining car, and passengers took the opportunity to stretch their legs, have a drink in the pub or dance to an African band on the station platform. In fact a good time was had by all.

Bulawayo, a railway and industrial centre, was then the largest town in Rhodesia. We arrived there early in the morning and I was met by the senior government medical officer, an exceptional, efficient and vigorous gentleman, who soon discovered we had qualified at the same London hospital. He informed me we were the only two in Rhodesia who had this fortunate advantage. I was presented with a large Ford sedan for my personal use and, almost immediately, was set to work examining army recruits. I was told that medical personnel were not being recruited into the Southern Rhodesia forces as yet, and that I would be employed as a government medical officer in Bulawayo pro tem. Later in the day he took me round the town visiting the hospitals, police station, gaol and other government institutions I would be visiting daily. The most striking feature about Bulawayo were the wide streets in the city centre. They were planned so that an ox wagon and team could turn round in them without difficulty. The European residential suburbs were very pleasant; the houses had large gardens facing quiet tree-lined avenues. It did not resemble an English town, but with its straight streets all running north to south or east to west with regular intersections, it was more typical of a South African town.

The next day I visited the gaol and first experienced the indignity of having to witness corporal punishment being administered. The prisoners, all black, who had been sentenced to lashes in the magistrates' court, were strapped to a special frame by their wrists and ankles. All the warders I had seen administering the lashes were obviously South Africans, physically big men, apparently selected for their strength and inclination. Bamboo canes were used. The buttocks of the strapped prisoners were painted with iodine and the warder took up a stance and used all the strength he had available to lash the buttocks. The cane came down with a swish and a large weal appeared where it met the buttocks. Blood was usually drawn. Most prisoners let out a yell as each lash was administered, but the more resolute or defiant did not utter a sound. As far as I can recollect, the average number of strokes administered was ten. I found the strain of having to witness the sadistic practice of lashing more irksome than attending hangings and, at times, felt more sorry for the individual wielding the cane than for the prisoner strapped to the frame at the receiving end. The obvious satisfaction shown in the faces and general demeanour of the European warders carrying out this administration of justice was revolting. I later learned that the previous medical officer to myself had become physically sick after his first attendance at a lashing session and flatly refused to attend another.

Later in the day I was instructed to carry out a postmortem examination on a body found in the bush near a place called Bembezi on the main Bulawayo to Salisbury road, about 40 miles from Bulawayo. The directions given me were to get onto the strip road near the gaol, which I had visited previously, and drive for about 30 miles and then proceed slowly because a policeman on a motorcycle would be waiting for me alongside the road. I found the strip road, which consisted of two tarmac or concrete strips, each about one and a half feet wide to accommodate the wheels of the motor vehicle, set in a gravel road. At first I found these strips difficult to negotiate at any speed, but soon learnt the secret of looking ahead and not down in front of the car, which was a natural inclination. When a vehicle approached travelling in the opposite direction, one had to move over to the left and each vehicle used one strip while passing. All the main roads in Southern Rhodesia were stripped and extended for several thousand miles throughout the territory. It is of interest to note that these roads had been constructed by European labourers during the depression in the first half of the decade. They were paid five shillings (25 pence) a day for their labour. The government considered it was more satisfactory for them to be usefully employed than to be given largesse or the modern equivalent of the dole.

To return to my trip to Bembezi to carry out the postmortem, I had driven 30 miles and then more slowly for another 20 miles, but did not see a policeman waiting by the roadside. In fact I did not see another vehicle, a living soul, or indeed even an animal along the road. Eventually I noticed a structure in the bush consisting of two upright posts with a metal stamp in between. I stopped and walked through the bush towards the structure and was met by a weather-beaten, bearded old man. He appeared as though he had not had an opportunity to wash or change his clothing for many days. It turned out he was engaged in running a one-man gold mine, crushing ore with the help of a couple of Africans and extracting any gold that may be there. I later discovered that this lone prospecting or mining of gold was not an unusual occupation in Rhodesia at that time. On my enquiring about Bembezi he became very amused and informed me that I should be on the Salisbury road. The road I was on led to the Lonely Mine. The only way to get to Bembezi was to return to Bulawayo and set out again on the Salisbury road. This I did and found that the Salisbury road left Bulawayo a short distance away from and at a different angle from the Lonely Mine road. It was an irate but respectful policemen I eventually found waiting at the roadside near Bembezi, which consisted of a couple of houses and a railway station. He had been waiting patiently for me for over three hours.

Holding my bag of instruments and balancing on the back of his motorcycle, we bumped along a bush path for about a mile, then abandoned the machine and walked through the trees for a short distance before reaching a wide circle of Africans sitting in a small clearing. A body lay in the centre of the circle. I had read about it, but this was the first occasion I had seen a death from electrocution by lightning. When the body had been undressed a burn was evident on his right thigh where his trouser pocket had contained silver coins. Another burn on his abdomen was immediately under the site of the metal buckle of his belt. Small haemorrhages on his lungs completed the picture of this typical textbook case. By the time I had finished my examination and was sewing up the body it was twilight. The African mourners, mostly women, had returned and, as was their custom, began a mournful wail. It was an eerie

27

experience and I was pleased to return to the comparative safety of my car. This was to be the first of many expeditions into the bush and I had a feeling of satisfaction that my anticipation of finding adventure was being realized.

From a professional point of view life could not have been more interesting or fulfilling. In addition to the innumerable medical and surgical cases we had to deal with in the African hospital — there were only three government medical officers in Bulawayo — we also had to attend to indigent Europeans, the police and school boarders, as well as to do medico-legal work, frequently appearing at inquests and giving evidence in assault, rape and other court cases. Many new and interesting medical conditions were found in African patients, but there was no time for academic research. One was expected to deal with all conditions. Consultants had not arrived on the scheme as yet, but a number of practitioners in the town had specialist interests such as ophthalmology or surgery, and their opinions were sought on occasion. The European population of Bulawayo was 13,000 and, from the outset, I found life there most desirable. Unlike South Africa, there was an overt friendly relationship between the races. The blacks treated the Europeans with abject respect, always giving way on the pavements and removing their hats when they passed in the streets. When they met a European in the countryside they would stand still, bow their heads and softly clap their hands in respect. I do not think this attitude was demanded of them. It was a natural gesture of recognition of racial superiority taking into account the relatively few whites in the territory and the wisdom and knowledge of these superior people who could understand machinery, cure their diseases, develop large farming estates and in fact were capable of unfathomable accomplishments. The African policemen were a fine, specially selected, smart body of men with exceptional physiques. I recollect that a common complaint among them was sore feet due to walking the beat barefoot on hard pavements. Medical certification was required to allow them to wear leather sandals while on duty.

Bulawayo, which is a derivation of the phrase '*bulala wayo*' or 'place of killing' in Ndebele, is the capital of Matabeleland in the southern half of the country. Its historical connection with Rhodes and Lobengula, the Matabele chief, and why it was called the 'place of killing' can be found recorded in many books. The Matabele, who originally came from the south and were an offshoot of the Zulu, spoke the Ndebele language and accounted for about one quarter of the native population of Southern Rhodesia.

Social life in Bulawayo was pleasant and people were exceptionally friendly. They had a free and easy attitude, as exemplified by a story a well-known judge told me about himself. He attended a dance given by a select social club where he met an acquaintance who offered him a glass of French champagne. He had half finished his champagne when his acquaintance quickly removed the glass from his hand, set it back on the table and made him move on quickly to another part of the hall. It appeared that the champagne he had been drinking did not belong to his acquaintance but to a party who had been dancing and were now returning to their table.

At weekends we played golf on a course with cinder greens, or went shooting for wild guinea fowl in the mostly flat bush countryside. I found its vast expanse fascinating. Sometimes we would visit and climb the Matopos Hills — an unusual granite outcrop of great beauty known as World's View, about 15 miles from the city, where Rhodes and other patriots were buried and which had become a European national shrine. It may seem unreasonable of me to distinguish persistently between European and black customs or spheres of interest, but one has to face the facts. In those days before the European influx into the territory, when the rise of African nationalism was not known and the white man's leadership was unquestioned, one was always conscious of the racial pattern in South and Central Africa.

A medical definition of the female sex states there are two types of female — those who are pregnant and do not wish to have a baby and those who wish to have a baby and are sterile. The same definition could be applied to Rhodesian males in a different connotation. Although there was conscription in Southern Rhodesia, in those early days of the Second World War there were many individuals, and I was one of them, who were agitating to get into the army but were unable to do so because of their occupation. There were others, but less numerous, who had been called up but who would have preferred to remain in civilian life. Many who were not conscripted joined the territorial forces. The general high calibre of the European male population made the recruits excellent officer material for African troops being mobilized in other African territories, such as Nigeria and the Gold Coast. Many were drafted to these countries as officers. A black Rhodesian regiment with white officers was later recruited and served in Malaya with distinction.

The longer I was in Bulawayo the more I enjoyed being there. Evenings were frequently spent in the bar of the hotel in which I lived or in the police mess. The police force in Rhodesia was known as the BSAP (British South African Police). It was a famous force of almost worldwide renown. Its members held army rank and policemen were known as troopers. They were selected for their background and had comparatively high educational qualifications. Practically all recruitment was in the United Kingdom. The out of town or district police did long patrols on horseback, sometimes lasting for weeks. Outlying farms or villages were visited periodically. A packhorse and African constable accompanied the patrolling trooper. Crime was comparatively infrequent and the attitude of the force was based on helpful cooperation with all races. They were unarmed and no shot had been fired by them in anger throughout the period from the inception of the force at the turn of the century. Indeed, I understand that the first time a firearm was used by the police against a lawbreaker was in 1960.

An elderly medical officer was appointed by the government at this time to carry out medico-legal work in the area. As his work was less demanding, his attendance at the hotel bar was more frequent and longer than my own. One Saturday night I was called on by the police to examine a man involved in a car accident who was thought to be under the influence of alcohol. I referred the police trooper to my recently appointed colleague, who eventually left the bar with an unsteady gait to carry out his duty. I regret I did not actually see the examination being conducted and considered it policy not to enquire too closely as to what happened, but one can well imagine the amusing sight of one unsteady

30

individual requesting another to walk along a straight line or say 'British Constitution'. Life in Rhodesia in those days was like that. Everyone seemed happy and unconcerned. Little episodes like the one mentioned would be thought of as amusing. In another country a similar episode would most likely be taken seriously with repercussions.

Despite the general carefree attitude, an early impression of Rhodesia was a marked efficiency in all walks of life. Government departments were well run and civil servants were obliging. It was not a rich territory but very high standards were maintained in the hospitals, schools, courts, police and other institutions. As stated before, there were no signs of friction or tension between the races, but there was also no obvious social mixing between them. African nationalism was not known or even anticipated and there were no prominent leaders in the African community. The European settlers were paternalistic and there was an even more rigid colour bar than in South Africa. It would have been unrealistic even to imagine multiracial public buses in a Rhodesian town, as there had been in Cape Town when I was a schoolboy. On the other hand, the black policeman on traffic point duty in Bulawayo would have been unthinkable in Cape Town. And, although the Rhodesian constitution did not disqualify people from the franchise on the grounds of race, as the South African one did, educational and financial qualifications were sufficiently high to ensure that very few Africans were entitled to vote.

The European settlers were in the main British. A proportion of them were South African, though I rarely heard Afrikaans being spoken in Bulawayo. Very few had been born in Rhodesia. They tended to work as skilled artisans, farmers, businessmen, or in the professions or civil service. A large proportion were in the employ of the railways. They were stoic independent-minded individuals, complacent but tough and earthy and, in general, were likeable people. Class distinction was not evident in the European community and, unlike in England or South Africa, there was no display of wealth, though the Bulawayo Club was an exclusive stronghold of the establishment. During the early part of the war white territorials, according to the local press, demonstrated against the establishment at the club. Indigent Europeans were few

and far between, but as government medical officers we were
sometimes called on to treat these folk, whom I personally
resented. There was no place for irresolute or fickle Europeans in a
vigorous young developing country. They lived in shanties at the
edge of the town and, despite their dreadful basic living conditions,
invariably had a large radio gramophone and a big American car,
paid for on the 'never never' system. Contrary to general belief, I
found that Rhodesians were not heavy drinkers. They consumed
large quantities of lager type beer, which was good but had a low
alcoholic content. Spirits were drunk slowly as long drinks with
large amounts of soda, water or tonic added to the tots. Although
the social habit of having a sundowner was à la mode, comparatively small amounts of alcohol were consumed at each session. It
was not unusual for Europeans to discuss race relations. On one
evening I was present when opinions were expressed as to how
long it would be before an African would be able to drive a motor
vehicle. One said 100 years. Others suggested it would take only
25 years or even 20 years. In fact they were driving cars and
heavy-duty vehicles within five years and one leading motor truck
manufacturer expressed the opinion that they were among the
most reliable drivers in the world.

The months passed and one of the other government medical
officers, who was a particular friend of mine, was suddenly transferred to Melsetter, a small town on the eastern border of the
territory, near Mozambique. It was beautiful mountainous country
but very isolated and practically all the residents in the area were
Afrikaners and English was rarely spoken. It is interesting to relate
that there were a number of small Afrikaner settlements, similar to
Melsetter, in various parts of Central Africa, and even further
north in Kenya. It appears that when the Boer War ended, with the
defeat of the Boers at the beginning of the century, numbers of
independent minded Boers or Afrikaners preferred not to remain
under British rule in South Africa and trekked north to find
pastures new. They formed small farming communities in pleasant
highland areas, chosen for a good climatic and agricultural potential. Those in Melsetter and Enkeldoorn in Southern Rhodesia are
there to this day, while others such as Eldoret in Kenya and the
outskirts of Lusaka in Zambia were evacuated with the advent of

independence. This is tragic because these early settlers were great pioneers who hacked farms out of bush land and were a credit to any country in which they settled. They retained their Calvinistic culture, Afrikaans language and paternalistic attitude to the Africans. The odd intrepid few who stayed on and did not sell or abandon their farms and return to South Africa have not been molested and were doing comparatively well.

A friend of mine who had come from England only a year previously was very unhappy in Melsetter. He returned to Bulawayo briefly to see his wife and baby and then decided to see the director of medical services in Salisbury, the capital city and seat of government, the next day to complain about his transfer to Melsetter at so short notice. I decided to accompany him and enquire about the delay in my being called up for military service. The director of medical services, we found, was a bloated, bluff autocrat who was unaware that my friend had been transferred. We discovered that a senior clerk was responsible for the deposition of government medical officers in the territory and he apparently had the authority to move them around like draughts on a board. Although it was not directly my business, this was my first experience of bureaucracy and there was a heated divergence of opinion. I returned to Bulawayo in the knowledge that I would not be a government medical officer much longer. I was not disappointed in my surmise, so I joined a private practice in Bulawayo and also became relief medical officer to the Rhodesian Railways.

While working as a railway medical officer I took the opportunity to travel on the pay train — a special train which ran from Bulawayo to Ndola on the Copperbelt in Northern Rhodesia at the beginning of each month. The train consisted of a guard's van, three special coaches and a number of covered goods wagons loaded with supplies for railway personnel along the line. The coaches were in turn occupied by a paymaster, a supplies clerk and the medical officer. The paymaster's coach was fitted out as a bank, with safes, banking hall, office and living quarters for the paymaster and his servant. The coach for the supplies clerk had an office and similar living quarters. The medical coach, the longest of the three, had a small waiting area, consulting room, dispensary and small operating room. The living quarters consisted of a sitting room, bedroom, bathroom (with full bath and shower) and a kitchen. There was a small compartment at the end for the African dispenser, who also acted as cook, waiter, interpreter and general factotum. The train stopped at all pump houses, gangers' cottages and sidings or stations wherever railway personnel were quartered. While the paymaster paid out employees and the supplies clerk distributed food and other stores, I attended the sick. Gangers, who were mostly married, lived in railway cottages every nine miles along the track. Each ganger had about ten African track labourers working under his supervision and they lived in a compound or collection of huts near his own cottage. Most of these gangers' or plate layers' cottages were very isolated, with no access by road, and the wives would invariably come out for a chat whether requiring medical attention or not. The opportunity to talk to a European, other than their husband or children, once a month was too good to be missed. I did the first section of the line from Bulawayo to Livingstone in Northern Rhodesia, a few miles beyond the Zambezi River and the Victoria Falls, and then returned to Bulawayo by mail train. The trip took two days from Bulawayo to Livingstone. The Victoria Falls was a most impressive sight and Livingstone, a very pleasant town, was reminiscent of a small English town transplanted to the tropics. I was entertained by the Livingstone Railway medical officer, who took over from me to work the pay train on the next section. I secretly hoped it would be possible for me to replace him one day in the future. This was my first visit to Northern Rhodesia, a colonial African territory administered by the Colonial Office in Whitehall.

Early in the new year I was awakened in the night and handed an urgent telegram, which informed me that I was now a member of His Majesty's Forces in the Rhodesian Medical Corps and that I should arrange to draw my uniform and kit at the Drill Hall that day and be prepared to leave for an unknown destination within 48 hours. The purpose for which I had come to Rhodesia had been fulfilled. I was issued with a car load of military kit and equipment from a canvas bath down to a toothbrush and comb. The military tailor took my measurements and by the next day my uniforms were ready. I sold my car and wireless set, the only tangible consumer goods I possessed, and was ready to leave. It would be wrong to deny how proud and important I felt to be wearing the uniform of a full lieutenant in His Majesty's Forces and to be smartly saluted by other ranks passing in the street. My untrained returned salute must have obviously been self-conscious and inadequate.

Before leaving Rhodesia I reflected on my impressions of the territory following my first few months' residence there. These were undoubtedly favourable towards the country and its inhabitants and transcended any happy anticipation I may have had before my arrival. The weather was agreeable and the country vast and captivating. Because of the happy, contented atmosphere evident among all races, one did not experience any perception of colonial conquest. The long established concept of the colonial settler wearing a pith helmet or a large bush hat, with a bottle of whisky in one hand and a *sjambok* in the other, was justified only with the wearing of a bush hat. The adherence of the majority of the European population to British traditions and justice made it all the more attractive from my own point of view. I did not know the proportion of British compared to South African and other residents, but anyone in the United Kingdom who referred to his 'kith and kin' in Rhodesia at that time was substantially correct in his phraseology.

Because of the pleasant attitude of the Africans, who did not appear to have any political opinions, I was not aware, as one should have been, of my privileged position as a European living in an African country. The Africans were willing, uncomplaining servants performing all kinds of menial jobs. The chauvinistic Europeans, with illogical obstinacy and with very few exceptions, did not trouble to learn or speak the local Ndebele language, but expected the Africans to understand and speak English, which many did well, especially in the towns. At times communication between the races was difficult. In government institutions such as hospitals, interpreters were used, but the most popular means of communication was by a type of pidgin English knows as 'Kitchen Kaffir' or '*Funagalo*' (do it like this). This was a jargon consisting of Ndebele, which was similar to Zulu, and English with a few Afrikaans words. It was easily learnt by all and, at times, tended to sound farcical. A typical example would be in the case of a European instructing an African assistant to perform some task — 'Yensa so gashla, no not so bloody gashla you mompara' (do this slowly, no not so slowly, you idiot). Language purists of both races strongly objected to the common use of this jargon. Of course no society can be perfect and in the course of my work I had become involved in many cases of cruelty to employees by employers, or to use a local description, to servants by masters. Most of these were cases of assault, but there were isolated instances of employees developing vitamin deficiency from inadequate feeding. At times one speculated on the fact that if these employees had been slaves, owned by their masters, more interest would have been taken in their welfare.

The day after receiving my telegram of commission I joined the company of the Rhodesian Medical Corps consisting of eight officers and 50 other ranks, and we left Bulawayo by special train for an unknown destination. Except for two other officers and myself, the rest of the unit had been training at a camp in Salisbury for some weeks. Within an hour of leaving Bulawayo, and this was really my first hour in the army, I had a depressed feeling of being back in boarding school once again. Our commanding officer was an old Indian Army medical officer, who had retired to Rhodesia and had been recalled to the colours. His stupid pomposity fulfilled my description of the type to be found in the pages of *Punch* or other humorous publications. Unfortunately we had to experience the reality of this despot who, after a few minutes of leaving Bulawayo, called us into his compartment and told us how to behave and show him due respect because of his rank. It was rumoured, but not confirmed, that we were on our way to East Africa via Durban in South Africa. We were on a special train consisting of goods trucks in the front and three passenger coaches and a dining car for our use at the rear. In the early hours of the next morning we arrived at Mafeking, the journey having taken three hours less than the scheduled fast mail train. The whole of the next day was spent in Mafeking where we were entertained at the club and also at a banquet given in our honour at the town hall following a march through the town centre. A speech given by the local commander of military forces was a masterpiece of non-commitment about his commitment to the war effort against Germany.

South Africa had by now declared war on Germany and we were informed that we were the very first troops — albeit a medical unit — to pass through or leave the country for the theatre of war. When we left for Johannesburg that night we were feted by many of the Mafeking residents. Boxes of fruit and chocolates, cigarettes, knitted socks and pullovers, and other presents were piled into our carriages in profusion. In an incredible succession of fast and slow journeys, with long or short stops in between, we eventually arrived at Durban and boarded the SS *Tirea*, a passenger liner of the British India Line bound for Bombay. The vessel was comparatively small but had four long funnels. This incongruous assembly of funnels was later explained by the ship's officers. Only one was used for emission of smoke while the others were dummies. Impossible as it may seem today, their passengers, who were mostly Indian, preferred to travel on a multi-funnel ship because of prestige and perhaps because they thought it was a sign of more power and safety.

The reason for the stop-and-go train journey was explained to me some years later. Attempts were made by pro-German elements in South Africa to sabotage troop trains, so erratic schedules were arranged for these trains at the last moment by a senior railway official in order to circumvent the saboteurs. My brother-in-law, who was in a South African armoured car unit, spent a long period of his military service in South Africa itself patrolling electrical power lines and other installations to prevent sabotage. I cannot vouch for the accuracy of the information but was also told that the large Cunard Queen liners, full of Australian troops on their way to the Middle East and other theatres of war, were never far from the South African coast during the first years of the war so that they would be available for immediate landing in the event of an uprising by the antiwar pro-Nazi element. After all, it should not be forgotten that a couple of South African prime ministers, in office in recent years, were active supporters of the Nazi regime before and during the war. It is a pity that no one, to my knowledge, has researched and recorded the background to the war effort in South Africa during the Second World War.

We sailed out of Durban harbour later that day. We, the officers, were accommodated as ordinary first-class passengers, while the other ranks were in tourist class. Our first port of call was Lourenço Marques, now known as Maputo, in Mozambique. As the Portuguese, who were the imperial power over Mozambique, had not joined in the war this was neutral territory. We were warned that German agents or spies were active in Mozambique and were not allowed ashore in uniform. We spent two days at the port and did go ashore in the evenings in civilian clothes borrowed from the ship's officers. We did the same at our next port of call which was Beira. In the meantime we were officially informed that we were on our way to Nairobi to open a base military hospital. Every morning we were instructed in army drill on deck by our sergeant major. The instructions always ended with a loud 'Sir'. The next port of call, Dar es Salaam in Tanganyika, was in British territory so there was no difficulty going ashore. It was a pleasant town with lazy palm and coconut tree-lined beaches. Imbibing cool beer in the evening in the gardens of the club, which overlooked the harbour, with the background music of a military band, had pleasurable appeal. The barman at the club was an unusual gentleman, who had an obvious military bearing and wore a monocle. The next time I met him was on Christmas Day when, as senior brigadier of the East African Army Headquarters Command, he paid an official visit to the military hospital where I had to escort him around. This was to be the first of many more encounters in Africa with individuals whose occupations were inconsistent with their dignity or background.

Our next port of call was Zanzibar, a delightful tropical island with a constant pervading odour of cloves, which grew there in profusion. During the day we spent there I took the opportunity to be measured for a silk tropical suit by an Indian tailor. For a negligible cost it was cut, stitched and fitted within a couple of hours — in your presence if you wished. The next day we disembarked at Mombasa and entrained for Nairobi. This was the only train I knew of that had a bottle opener fixed to the wall of each compartment. Early the next morning we awoke to discover we were passing through a game reserve; as we steamed along and the abundance of game — antelope, giraffe, ostrich and even

38

lion — came into view, the carriage window took on the appearance of a modern coloured television screen.

As soon as we arrived in Nairobi, we got down to opening a base military hospital for the impending East African campaign. A hospital for non-European troops had already been established by an East African medical corps unit. It is not my intention to describe in any detail my experiences in the army during the next few years. It was inconvenient because it interrupted my career. I did not see a shot fired in anger but travelled over a large area of Africa at His Majesty's expense. Nairobi was an exceptionally attractive town and had ample facilities for entertainment with super clubs, hotels and restaurants. Most sports were readily available. We were made honorary members of the Nairobi Club and the cheap crustacean seafoods, such as lobster or prawns, brought up from the coast in large quantities, were an unexpected bonus. I recently visited Nairobi and it has changed little during the past 35 years. There were obvious dissimilarities when compared to Southern Rhodesian towns. The Indian influence was noticeable in banks, where all the tellers were Indians, in the building and other industries practically all artisans were Sikhs, and the majority of shops, garages and other commercial enterprises were Indian owned.

The attitude of the indigenous Kenya Africans was quite different from that in Southern Rhodesia. They were more advanced, more independent, less docile and obsequious and there was an indefinable sense of hostility toward Europeans, which became apparent soon after our arrival. They did not speak English and we had to take a crash course in Swahili, a comparatively easy language to learn, as it was incumbent upon Europeans in Kenya to converse with Africans in their own language. Their manners were impeccable, but petty thieving was a prevalent nuisance, which I was to discover later is an early symptom of impending change in an African territory.

The local European population did not impress me. A large number of settlers were said to be remittance men and, if one were to believe news reports in the local newspapers, their moral standards were subnormal. The exaggerated attitude of superiority as observed in the clubs left one with a sense of inevitable change in the future. Perhaps the rise of the Mau Mau and almost revolutionary change to African independence in Kenya was not fortuitous.

I was indeed fortunate to be in the army and have the opportunity to work in a base hospital. The hospital had been open a matter of days when South African troops in their thousands began to arrive in Nairobi in road convoys from Broken Hill in Northern Rhodesia. Their air force was also established in Nairobi. Nearly all our patients were South Africans, with odd British personnel and European colonials, attached to the many battalions of the King's African Rifles from various African colonial territories then stationed in Kenya. The few Italian prisoners of war I attended as patients were pathetic. They spent a large part of their time looking at photos of their families with tears rolling down their cheeks.

This was during the battle for Britain and any spare time we had, and there was little, was spent in front of a radio listening with glee to news about the increasing numbers of German aircraft being brought down over England each day. The East African campaign in Abyssinia was beginning to 'hot up' and we had difficulty coping with ever increasing numbers of patients being admitted with tropical and other medical complaints. The work was demanding and interesting, and the frail nature of human endeavour under stress soon became a difficult problem. It became evident that, under the circumstances, disease as we then saw it was often an attitude of mind to real or imagined symptoms. For instance, there was the case of a soldier with severe pulmonary tuberculosis, with both lungs largely destroyed, who had spent many months fighting under adverse conditions in the desert or bush, who had been brought back to base against his will and whose only thought was to get back to the front again as soon as possible. On the other hand, there were many with trivial complaints who were returned to base for treatment time and again, but were quite incapable of carrying on in combatant units because of irresolution or infirmity of purpose. There were numerous cases of hysterical paralysis. A South African psychiatrist, who had originally come from Holland, was attached to our unit and his help in sorting out these cases was invaluable.

He often used, and taught me how to use, mesmerism in the treatment of hysterical paralysis, with invariably good results provided the right patients were chosen to be put in a trance. The reaction of these patients who found they could suddenly use their limbs again when they came out of the trance was surprising and amusing. All sorts of reasons were given for their recovery and a large number said it was due to a correspondence course they were taking with a well-known physical culturist who blatantly advertised in many South African newspapers. No wonder he was able to display many letters of commendation from his clients in these advertisements. One of my many more unpleasant duties was to look after military personnel in the local mental hospital, which was largely handed over to us for military use. These were the days before the advent of psychotropic drugs and many patients were confined to padded cells.

An irritating duty we had to perform was the perusal of all mail written by patients under our care. Most of the letters were to wives or girlfriends and consisted of unadulterated sex, explaining in lurid detail what they intended to do when they returned home after their long abstemious absence. We were requested by military intelligence to look out for cases of men who were concerned by the non-payment of pay to wives and dependants at home. In the course of censoring letters, numbers of these cases were detected and, as a result, a conspiracy of the antiwar pro-German element of South Africa was discovered. Anonymous letters were sent to South African soldiers, usually signed by 'an interested neighbour', informing them that their wives and children were starving at home because of non-payment of their allotment. This was intended and was effective in undermining the morale of the troops.

Life in the army was carefree and could be amusing at times. The dentist attached to our unit was an old bachelor, very Scottish, and a keen amateur actor who would perform a monologue on Valhalla at the slightest provocation. His devotion to the histrionic arts appeared to be proportional to the amount of whisky consumed. His surgery was next to mine and, one morning after an exceptionally heavy night, he was attending to the teeth of the officer commanding the troops in the East African campaign. The general, noticing the tremor in his hands, requested him to stop

41

operations and to imagine he was treating an ordinary private. According to my dentist friend it was just as well that the general's diagnosis was at fault. I still laugh to myself every time I recollect the telling of this episode by our dramatic dental colleague.

One day all medical personnel concerned were instructed to attend a meeting addressed by the officer commanding South African troops. He informed us that the South African army was a volunteer force and that he would rather have 10,000 keen men under his command than 100,000 hangers on. He requested us to ensure that men who were continually being brought to the base for medical or other reasons should be boarded back to South Africa without delay. As a result of this command it was not long before train loads of South African troops were being sent home via Mombasa. It was never quite clear why these men volunteered for military service in the first instance.

The Kenya countryside was delightful, with all sorts of game to be seen near and even in Nairobi. It was not unusual to see antelope and other wild animals in the hospital grounds. We motored into the Rift Valley and the Masai, or 'warrior tribe', seen there were an interesting people. They were tall and thin and lived entirely off the livestock they possessed. We were told that the men had to kill a lion armed only with a spear in order to prove their manhood. Unlike the women folk in the Rhodesias, who carried water containers, wood and other goods on their heads with graceful ease, the women of the Kikuyu tribe were like beasts of burden. These women, and some were very old, could be seen in the countryside carrying their burdens on their backs, held there by a leather thong or strap that passed around their foreheads. Some of the loads they carried were awesome and they walked in a forward leaning position as they strained under the burden. Many of the women had permanent marks in their foreheads from the pressure of the strap. I found these human beasts of burden a very unpleasant sight.

The coffee farms near Nairobi, and other European farms in the Highlands of Kenya, appeared to be prosperous with attractive homesteads and surroundings. The countryside was more lush and green than it was in Rhodesia and at times was reminiscent of England. While stationed in Nairobi, a colleague and myself spent a week in Uganda visiting the Yellow Fever Research Institute and other places of interest. We were invited to a banquet in Entebbe — I cannot remember the occasion — but do remember it was an official function and all guests were seated according to their rank or rate of pay in the colonial government hierarchy. We also attended an international soccer match between Kenya and Uganda, held at a sports stadium in Kampala. The players did not have the benefit of wearing boots and I was intrigued to see how hard and far they could 'boot' the ball with their bare feet. I mention this event because the spectators, all black, with only the odd European face in the crowd, were exceedingly well turned out. The women were in long flowing dresses and the men in neat suits. It reminded me of a less sophisticated version of an Ascot fashion parade. The Ugandan Africans appeared to be by far the most advanced I had seen in Africa. Their huts or kraals, with the inevitable banana palms in the vicinity, were much cleaner and neater than any I had seen in other territories.

The so-called 'African problem' was occasionally discussed with residents in Nairobi. A local doctor informed me that the Masai were quite happy if left alone and that the Kikuyu, the majority of local Africans, were the rogues of Africa. By this he meant that they were only interested in money and would never fight for their rights. How wrong he was! Within a few years the Mau Mau, who were Kikuyu, had established themselves and showed that eventually even the 'worm will turn'.

The East African campaign was now coming to an end and our unit was being split up. Japan was in the war and there was fear of an attack on southern Africa via Madagascar, now known as Malagasy. One day I was told by my commanding officer that I would be returning to Southern Rhodesia within a week. I flew back to Broken Hill from Nairobi in a South African Air Force plane. It was a Lodestar, then the most modern of all transport aircraft with an impressive silvery shiny body. The crew referred to it as a flying coffin. The only other passenger was a South African medico who, more acquisitive than myself, was returning with a German Mauser rifle and an assortment of expensive medical instruments he had 'won' in the course of his medical service in Kenya. At one stage of the flight the engine stopped without warning and, without panic, I really thought the end had come. In the unwelcome silence I looked down on the thick bush covering the country as far as the eye could see. A sergeant came out of the door leading to the flight deck and casually explained that this was the only craft in which it was possible to 'feather' the engines in flight and this was a demonstration. The engines were then started up again. We lost no time in telling him that the passengers were entitled to be told about the demonstration before and not after the event. We landed on a small airfield at Dadoma in Tanganyika, where a terrific cooked breakfast was supplied free by the local ladies as part of their war effort, and we came down at Mbeya in Northern Rhodesia, where a poor lunch was supplied at exorbitant cost by the local hotelier as part of his war effort. We landed at Broken Hill in Northern Rhodesia, the railhead from South Africa which had been developed as the army base for the East African campaign. All road convoys and transport aircraft left from there for the north. We had to spend two days in a local hotel waiting for the train to Salisbury, which ran only three times a week. I strolled around the town and noticed the railway medical officer's house facing the park. Little did I realize I would be occupying this residence in the comparatively near future.

On the long train journey from Broken Hill to Salisbury via Bulawayo I reflected on my stay in Kenya. I had been there for about 18 months and was pleased to be back in the Rhodesias. The African population in Kenya was obviously unsettled and the European settlers did not appeal to me as a type. They could be described as upper-middle-class people who were unable to make a 'go' of life in England and had found their niche in Kenya where they overtly enjoyed the *dolce vita*. Of course all generalizations are dangerous and I would like to point out that I am merely stating my own personal impression of Kenya as I found it after my period of residence there in the army. The majority of military personnel I met there were South Africans and I realized what a fine body of men they were. Granted they were a selected group who had volunteered for military service abroad, but they were tough reliable soldiers who shunned hypocrisy, were keen to get on with the job, finish it and get back home. They usually had a sense of humour and I never heard politics being discussed by them.

On arrival at Salisbury I was attached to the local military barracks as the medical officer in charge. After a few weeks of living in a tent we moved into the new officers' mess, which was luxurious by any standard and, as a result, my army pay was substantially lower than my mess bill.

Southern Rhodesia had changed during the time I had been up north. The Royal Air Force had arrived and was opening up training bases in Salisbury, Gwelo and Bulawayo and the influx of thousands of men and masses of equipment resulted in unaccustomed activity and prosperity, especially in the above centres. Salisbury's European population now equalled that of Bulawayo. The settled European population and better race relations were noticeable following my stay in Kenya. Hotels, pubs and other places of public entertainment were crowded and, despite the war, there was a pervading atmosphere of contentment and affluence. The invasion of Rhodesia by the Royal Air Force, which found the territory ideal for training its air crews because of the climate and easy availability of food and other resources, was a godsend for Rhodesia at the expense of the British taxpayer. There were no apparent shortages of any commodities or food; I was able to purchase a Chevrolet car at prewar prices and luxuries such as whisky and other alcoholic drinks were freely available. One had a deep regard for the intrepid merchant seamen who risked their lives daily to deliver the goods.

A frequent visitor to our mess was Sir Herbert Stanley, the governor-general of Southern Rhodesia. He took a genuine interest in the welfare of our troops and, on any occasion, was an outstanding speaker, which I first noticed when he officially opened our new military barracks and officers' mess. As I was to discover later he was the first of many famous men I would have the opportunity to meet in Central Africa. Within a few months I represented the medical corps at his farewell parade on Salisbury station and was sorry to see this erudite great leader leave the territory. He was one of the few prominent men who, in my experience, fully matched up to their responsibilities.

During the next couple of years I was stationed at various military establishments in the territory. I served for a period as regimental medical officer to the Rhodesia African Rifles, the first

African battalion recruited in Rhodesia. On one occasion I was sent to Durban with another officer and a company of men to escort Rashid Ali and his government colleagues from a ship in Durban harbour to Salisbury, where they were to be interned during the war for their anti-British activities. They brought their country's cash with them in wooden cases with unlocked lids (which were kept in our compartment) containing thousands of pounds in gold coins, mostly sovereigns, American 100-dollar notes and packs of other reliable currencies, such as Swiss francs and British five-pound notes. As far as I know nobody troubled to count all this money as there was far too much of it. We signed a receipt stating we had received so many thousands in cash, and obtained a similar receipt from the officer who admitted it to the detention centre. I often wondered what happened to all this cash of questionable ownership.

While at a military camp near Salisbury, where live shells were being fired by the artillery in training, I was behind the firing 25-pound field guns with the commanding officer. We were standing alongside what I thought was an old tree trunk when it suddenly began to move. We noticed it at the same moment and were momentarily rooted to the ground in fear — at least I was. It was the largest water python I had ever seen. Hearing our yelling, a couple of gunners with an axe chased it into a thicket and managed to behead it. The flaying undulating coils of the monster were a fascinating sight. It was 18 feet long, thick in proportion and it took more than ten men eventually to hold it down and transport it back to camp on a truck. Until that evening, six hours later, the coils went into action whenever the body of the reptile was touched, despite its headless condition. I was intrigued to see how long it took for the reflex nervous system to become inert. The next day we declined the offer of a python steak for dinner but were told that some of the troops had eaten the delicacy, which was said to have a similar taste to chicken.

On my first leave I motored down to Johannesburg. A circular from military headquarters stated that a passport was not necessary if travelling to South Africa in uniform. At the border an Afrikaans immigration official asked me for my passport, which I had with me but refused to produce, and referred him to the fact that I was in uniform. He muttered something in Afrikaans about my being a bloody *rooinek* — an objectionable Afrikaans description of an Englishman, which literally means redneck, derived from the sunburnt necks of the British soldiers in the Boer War. I made a suitable unprintable reply and drove through the border gate, my unshown passport in my pocket. It was during this leave that I met a young lady in Johannesburg who was serving as an officer in a part-time unit in the South African army. I am happy to say she is my 'superior' officer to this very day! Some months later our honeymoon was spent in Durban.

We returned to Gwelo where we had a hectic social life. Many Royal Air Force families of officers permanently in charge of training had come out from the United Kingdom and there was a happy crowd stationed there. A number of these personnel and their wives were ex-theatrical folk and, as a result, we were able to see shows of London West End standard put on by the local Green Room Club.

The army effort was now beginning to run down in Rhodesia and I was asked if I was willing to be demobilized to rejoin the Rhodesia Railways permanently at Broken Hill in Northern Rhodesia, where a railway medical officer was urgently required. It was stressed that I would be helping the war effort in a more useful capacity up there. After a verbal promise had been given that a transfer to Livingstone would be made when the first vacancy occurred, I had no hesitation in accepting the offer. We were unable to purchase what we required in Rhodesia but, being a railway official, a covered truck was placed at our disposal in Johannesburg, from where we made a special trip to purchase our requirements. This was sent off on the 1500-mile trip to Broken Hill, together with my car in another open truck, and within a few days, we were on our way. My career in Central Africa was about to begin.

3

Northern Rhodesia:
Broken Hill

B roken Hill, the railway centre of Northern Rhodesia, resembled a Wild West town as portrayed in American films. The main street, with irregular single-storeyed shops along one side of the thoroughfare and Boons Bar, with swing doors in their midst, looked as though it was a set erected for a cowboy film and at any moment one expected to see a gun-happy horseman riding into town. But any similarity to an American Wild West town was rather dissipated when a local resident pointed out that the iron triangle in front of the bar was sounded when a lion was spotted in the centre of the town as a warning to residents to take cover. Fortunately it had not been necessary to use it for some years.

The European population was about 6000 and the town was divided into three distinct residential areas — a railway camp, a mining camp and a much smaller area for other residents who were mostly engaged in commerce. Senior railway officials, including myself, all lived in fine houses in a select part of the town, mine officials in a special area in their own camp, and senior government officials lived in a small camp known as the Old Boma, or fort, about three miles outside the town limits. The house provided for the railway medical officer was a most impressive old colonial type of residence, completely surrounded by a gauze-enclosed veranda, and was large enough to ensure that a guest had his or her own suite with bathroom. The ceilings were exceptionally high, with double windows, and all floors were rendered cement over concrete. The lounge and dining room were so large that the truck load of furniture we had brought with us, adequate for any average home, looked completely lost in this rambling mansion. We wondered how we would ever cope with living in this empty attractive home, but there was no need to worry because we noted that in Northern Rhodesia there was no social kudos to be gained from possessing expensive furnishings. Mining and government officials had their furniture supplied to them and most of it was crude, made from indigenous hardwoods and leather thongs. After attending a couple of house sales we had ample cheap furniture and carpeting. Everyone was friendly and helpful and we soon settled down to our new life.

It did not take me long to find out how I would be helping in the war effort by working on the railway in Broken Hill. Rhodesia Railways, a British company, operated from Beira in Mozambique to the Copperbelt in Northern Rhodesia as one unit, and staff were freely transferable in the various territories. Imports were brought up from Beira and copper taken down there — a distance of some 1500 miles — for export mostly to England. This, with coal carried from Wankie collieries to the copper mines in Northern Rhodesia and the Belgian Congo and to power stations north and south, made up the bulk of the rail traffic. To the north the line connected up with the railway system in the Congo and from Bulawayo to the south it connected up with South African Railways. There was a saying in Northern Rhodesia at the time that the railways were the country because there was little to be found in the territory outside the line of rail. Roads were all dirt, corrugated and mostly impassable during the rainy season, and there was no regular air service. Except for missionaries, government servants and the odd farmer, all Europeans lived along the line of rail. Any conurbation that could rejoice under the name of a town was also on the railway line. In addition to moving general and passenger traffic, it was essential to get the copper through as quickly as possible for use in manufacturing munitions, aircraft and other necessities for sustaining the war effort in England.

As previously stated, there was conscription in Rhodesia during the war, but there was a choice open to conscripts — they could serve on the railways rather than join the army if they so desired. The result was that the majority of Afrikaners resident in the Rhodesias, especially those with anti-British inclinations, chose to join the railways. It was not possible to know how many, but a number of railway firemen stationed in Broken Hill were unhappy to realize that they were serving the war effort more usefully than if they had joined the armed forces.

The single-track railway running to the south from the Copperbelt and Congo was worked to full capacity within the constraints of engine power, availability of rolling stock, traffic density and, most important of all, the ability of personnel to cope. The trains' timetable, regulated by the number of crews available, was altered almost hourly during the night and day to ensure that the maximum number of trains would run. The train crews, who were on a seven-day rota, worked all hours of the day and night, and trains even ran on Christmas Day. Although their work was demanding and strenuous, their earning capacity was high because of overtime. Sometimes as many as ten firemen would book off sick in a row and this would lead to the cancellation of trains. Firemen to whom I had refused to issue sick certificates frequently appeared before the local magistrates' court on charges of malingering, under the manpower regulations. Within a few weeks after my arrival in Broken Hill my sick round included a visit to the local gaol where numerous railway employees were imprisoned.

I do not think the unhappy position at Broken Hill during this period has ever been fully recorded. About ten firemen, who had outstanding physiques, shaved their scalps and intentionally organized themselves into an anti-social group. Malingering was rife, fighting in public places such as bars and the local hotel when dances were held was commonplace, and I was personally threatened by this mob and warned by an anonymous caller on the telephone that I would be dealt with physically if my refusal to issue medical booking-off certificates continued. My wife was worried whenever I went out on a call after darkness had fallen. Events came to a head when a large flag with a swastika was tied to the spire of the Church of England church and swastikas were cut into the leather seats of cars parked outside the church during a Sunday morning service. The acts committed by these louts became incomprehensible when they were interviewed individually, for intrinsically they were decent lads. To my amazement one of them, an Afrikaner whom we considered to be the leader, joined the British Navy and, I understand, his war service was exemplary. Their spirit was eventually broken.

We had been in Broken Hill a couple of weeks when the junior government medical officer stationed there informed me that the provincial commissioner felt he had been slighted because I had been discourteous in not paying him an official visit, but that he would be pleased to see my wife and myself at his residence in the Old Boma the following evening for sundowners. I did not know what a provincial commissioner was, but an explanation by the medical officer made me realize that the invitation was a command rather than a request.

Northern Rhodesia was a colonial territory administered by the Colonial Office in Whitehall. The head and commander in chief of the territory was the governor followed by the chief secretary who, with other exalted gentlemen, were stationed at the secretariat in the capital city of Lusaka. The country was divided into provinces — I think there were six in the case of Northern Rhodesia — each governed by a provincial commissioner who was head of administration in his province. A varying number of district commissioners and district officers, most junior of all, served under the provincial commissioner. All these gentlemen, from the governor down to the usually young and inexperienced district officers, formed the nucleus of the administration in each colonial territory. They were, on the whole, a fine body of administrators, appointed in the United Kingdom and obviously specially selected. All those I met and knew had university degrees and most were educated at public schools. All had attended a course in administration at Oxford or Cambridge. These were the colonial servants who attended official functions in white tunics and feathered cocked hats, who wore spurs and sported swords.

The provincial commissioner had his office in the *boma* in the provincial town, which, in the case of the middle province, was Broken Hill. It was usually the outstanding building in the area with the Union Jack prominently displayed. Besides accommodating provincial government administrative offices, the *boma* also housed the local law courts. Junior employees such as typists and clerks were recruited locally, but senior clerks were often expatriates recruited in the United Kingdom. *Boma*s under district commissioners or district officers were located at convenient sites in the province and each officer had district messengers serving under him at his *boma*. These messengers, who wore distinctive navy blue and red uniforms, were Africans who acted as interpreters and had the power to arrest. They accompanied provincial officers on tours and acted as court orderlies. They were an especially loyal force with an outstanding *esprit de corps* and were completely trustworthy in their service to the Crown; all provincial officers were very dependent on their help.

The provincial commissioner represented the Crown in his area and was the senior civil servant responsible for the issue of licences and the collection of taxes in the rural areas. In bigger towns such as Broken Hill there was a visiting stipendiary magistrate from the Department of Justice, but all provincial officials were magistrates and, in some areas, the district commissioner or district officer was the magistrate, prosecutor, defence lawyer and perhaps even the chief gaoler. Provincial commissioners were also political agents and dealt with local problems. For instance on the Copperbelt he had to deal with industrial relations and in Barotseland would be associated with the king of the Barotses. They had an air of superiority and were generally unpopular among civil servants in other departments and non-government European residents. I thought this was due to envy because of their exalted position and the serene superiority some of them exuded. The fact that they came into contact with and frequently helped the African population did not encourage the Europeans to hold them in popular esteem.

The provincial administration has been described in some detail because this department was the core of British colonial administration in Africa. In the years to come I was to have frequent dealings with provincial and district commissioners in the course of my work and also in our social life. I have no hesitation in expressing the view that Britain can be proud of the administration provided at ground level in her African colonial territories. Of course it was inevitable that there were instances of maladministration and cases of personal inadequacy could be cited, but to this day many Africans will admit how they miss the advice and help of these colonial servants who left at the time of independence. They taught and were an example to the developing African of honest endeavour, dignity and, above all, justice. Perhaps they were better suited to bygone days when their tours and contacts with rural African chiefs and headmen were more leisurely. One experienced provincial commissioner told me shortly before he left how an African chief complained to him that, in the past, days were spent in his village discussing his problems, but now he only knew the commissioner 'by the dust of his departing Land-Rover'.

To return to our invitation to have sundowners at the residence of the provincial commissioner at the Old Boma near Broken Hill, in accordance with Southern Rhodesian custom we duly arrived there shortly after 6.00 p.m. and had instructed our cook to have our dinner ready at 8.00 p.m. We were admitted by a servant who informed us that the *bwana* and *dona* were dressing and were not ready to receive us. Having signed the visitors' book we self-consciously sat in his veranda lounge reading the usual English weekly periodicals for over half an hour until the commissioner and his attractive young wife appeared and welcomed us. He readily accepted my apologies for not being aware of local custom and for our unexpectedly early arrival. At the stroke of 7.00 p.m. the government medical officer arrived as a guest and, following a pleasant sundowner session, at about 7.45 p.m. we stood up, suitably thanked our host and hostess and announced that we would be leaving. He requested us to sit down and have another drink. He also said that he did not expect us to leave before 9.00 p.m. I explained that our cook expected us back by 8.00 p.m. and were sorry that we had to go. He curtly replied, 'If you leave now, you do so at my displeasure!' It then dawned on me that he was deadly serious and that his request for us to stay was a command. I could feel the shackles rising, but did not say another word and we left eventually to have our dinner on time. The next day I was told by our government medical officer friend that we had 'blotted our copybook' and were *personae non gratae* with the chief citizen — an inauspicious beginning to our stay in Northern Rhodesia. We soon found we were in good company as the American general manager of the mine and other leading residents were in the same position. For the next year until our pompous friend was transferred, we were left out of all official government functions.

Social life in Broken Hill was hectic. Shooting expeditions in the bush, where game was plentiful, and tennis parties at the railway, mine, government camps or surrounding farms occupied our time fully at weekends. Sundowner parties were almost a nightly ritual and we learnt to arrive and leave later, as was the custom. The African population was docile and Europeans were expected to have servants, whom their employers would feed, clothe and house in rooms in the backyards of their houses. We employed a cook boy, waiter boy, houseboy and garden boy, as they were called, to attend to the needs of the two of us. Their pay was a mere pittance. They were excellent servants; they did not object to the usual late dinners at about 9.30 p.m. and would willingly stay up all hours of the night if a party was held at home.

In retrospect it seems incredible that one was able to live so well for so little. Food, drink and all other goods were incredibly cheap and plentiful. I did a monthly trip on a special pay train, mentioned previously, on my section of the line from Kafue to the Copperbelt. Platelayers or gangers along the line frequently brought large quantities of tropical fruits and fresh and dried game meat, the latter known as *biltong*, to my coach. Vegetables were purchased at a siding called Kafulafuta, where the fertile soil had an ample water supply. For the standard price of sixpence (2½p), a large maize bag full of vegetables, which sometimes included tomatoes, cabbages or cauliflowers, could be purchased. A fat-tail sheep 'on the hoof' could be obtained for as little as half a crown (25p). Fresh eggs at three pence (1½p) a dozen and free-range chickens at sixpence (2½p) each were readily available. Each month when I returned to Broken Hill from the trip north, my car was completely filled with fresh foodstuff, which lasted until the next trip. One of the local stores had prewar bottles of French champagne, liqueurs and other luxury goods sold at prewar prices. In brief, we were able to live the luxurious life of a millionaire without having the means to pay for it.

Living in Central Africa during the latter part of the war and subsequently gave me a unique opportunity to observe and experience political, economic and social change from a simple practical point of view. For example, the sale and purchase of cheap basic foodstuffs came to an abrupt end about a year later, and Indian merchants began to buy up all the vegetables in Kafulafuta to sell at vastly increased prices in their shops. A local shopkeeper had the bright idea of sending his African employees out to purchase all the eggs being brought into the town along the three roads leading into Broken Hill. As a result housewives were forced to purchase eggs from his store at many times the original cost in the country area. This was the beginning of a change in the distribution of goods, or merchant trade, that benefited the middleman at the expense of the consumer. There were three European-owned general stores in the town and cheap prices came to an end when the owners or managers met each week and fixed the prices of most goods to ensure a fair profit and avoid undue competition. This was the beginning of a monopoly and the end of competitive capitalism in the town.

There were a variety of bizarre characters living in or near Broken Hill. An elderly lady, dressed up and looking like a dowager countess, could often be seen being carried majestically through the streets on a *machila*, a type of sedan chair on a bicycle wheel, suspended on a long pole supported on the shoulders of two African servants, one in front and the other in the rear. We became used to the sight but newcomers to the town simply stopped and stared in amazement. A ganger or platelayer stationed a few miles north lived a lonely life with his wife in a secluded little cottage alongside the railway track. On my monthly visits there on the pay train I was always impressed by his unusual command of the English language and obviously educated background. It was rumoured that he was a 'defrocked' English barrister, or whatever name is given to a lawyer who loses his licence to practise. He was offered promotion to the grade of permanent way inspector who supervises platelayers. His letter to the district engineer declining the promotion, on the grounds that he considered himself to be inadequate to undertake the added responsibility, was a masterpiece of sarcasm. Two cottages further along the track, which were spaced at nine-mile intervals, an extroverted fine specimen of a man with an odd Oxford/Afrikaans accent, told me how he spent all his spare time shooting in the bush. He made the best game *biltong* I have ever tasted but must have had other interests because on one trip I was approached by two young African women who complained that they were the master's wives and now that he had introduced another wife into the household the atmosphere was far from happy. They were disappointed when it was explained to them, through an interpreter, that I was unable to help them. Another young African girl, standing nearby quietly listening to the complaint, was apparently the third wife. The engine driver of a goods train reported an unusual episode. At about 3.00 p.m. on a Sunday afternoon, while travelling on an isolated part of the run between Kapiri Mposhi and Ndola, a middle-aged couple, both dressed in full evening dress, were observed walking alongside the track. On stopping and enquiring, the gentleman explained he was the local ganger and he and his wife were airing their garments, which they had not worn for years!

There were four fully-qualified civil engineers employed by the railways and stationed in Broken Hill. The chief engineer, who had been a mathematician, spent most of his time travelling up and down the line in his motor trolley inspecting the track and installations. He told me of an interesting episode. Apparently there was a difference of opinion between the government department concerned and himself about the siting of a new pumping station and tank for the supply of water to locomotives. Despite numerous letters and phone calls no agreement could be reached. When he was passing through Lusaka, the capital city, he phoned the government department concerned and the civil servant who answered the phone had full knowledge of the problem and suggested to the engineer that he come to his office where it could be finalized.

A car was hired and on arrival at the government offices, about two miles away from the railway station, he was astounded to discover that he had been talking to an African who settled the disagreement forthwith. This was a significant lesson in race relations.

The most junior young engineer, who was an Oxbridge graduate, was a pleasant extrovert who persisted in stating he was involved in every engineering prospect mentioned. One of his colleagues took the trouble to write down his engineering experiences and the time spent on them each time he related his story. At the end of about a year he produced the list he had recorded, which showed that the young man was nearly 100 years old. At that time a large photograph on the front page of the local press showed the officials responsible for the building of a large new brewery at Ndola, on the Copperbelt. In the front row our young friend was shown and recorded as the consulting engineer to the brewery firm. His colleagues were more upset than the culprit at this revelation. He resigned from the post as a railway engineer before his inevitable dismissal.

The monthly trips on the pay train made a pleasant break from routine. Someone invariably sought medical aid when we stopped at platelayers' or pumpers' cottages. The extraction of African employees' teeth without an anaesthetic — there was usually insufficient time to allow for a local anaesthetic to take — was done at most stops. I now recall this sadistic procedure with horror. We often travelled in or had meals in each other's coaches and, although it was contrary to regulations, I often acted as fireman or drove the engine. It was a thrill to have the sensation of power at my command when I operated the regulator or 'gun' and so increased the pulling power of the huge steam locomotive. It was necessary to know the track so that one could give the engine more 'gun' before coming to an incline, for if the increased power was not given when the incline had been reached the driving wheels would slip on the rails and the train could easily come to a standstill. Brakes had to be applied early on a downward slope so that the heavy train did not take curves at speed. One had to get used to the queer sensation of negotiating curves, for the bogies followed the line of the curve while the superstructure of the engine went straight on, with the bogies following along later. This gave the sensation of being derailed at each curve.

There was only one station between Ndola and Broken Hill and this was called Kapiri Mposhi. This is at present the railhead of the line constructed by the Chinese from Dar es Salaam in Tanzania to Zambia. The station was sited where the Great North Road to Cairo joined the road from the south and the Copperbelt. The 'city' of Kapiri Mposhi consisted of four railway houses for the stationmaster and three railway foremen who had to man the station and control the running of trains for 24 hours a day, seven days a week. There was also a small hotel, run by an ex-army major. One of the more unusual sights was to get there early enough in the morning to see him drilling his African staff. They all had to line up with broomsticks and were put through the usual military drill each day. The major, who was a tall elderly military gentleman, considered this instilled a sense of discipline into his staff. We invariably purchased a case of beer at his hotel to sustain us on the long journey to Ndola.

Something always seemed to be happening at Kapiri Mposhi. We were usually welcomed when we arrived there if for no other reason than that the employees received their monthly pay. On one occasion the station was deserted. On stepping down from my coach I noticed the station foreman's office was full of railway employees, who then gesticulated that we get back on the train and pointed ahead. We were just in time to see a huge lion strolling off the station platform. A regular sight was a dignified-looking gentleman invariably turned out in an immaculate lounge suit and grey trilby hat which would have been more in place in Bond Street. He was a retired district commissioner who ran a citrus farm in the district and was said to have a number of African wives. One night I was called out to Kapiri Mposhi to see a station foreman's wife who had developed blackwater fever — an interesting and deadly complication of malaria among irregular takers of quinine, which is now only of historical interest. It was a condition in which the red blood cells broke up and the resultant debris blocked the kidney tubes. Severe anaemia and heart failure were not unusual complications in these cases and their removal to hospital for treatment was always a problem. She was a heavy women and we were lifting her on a stretcher through a window into the compartment of a railway carriage on a train proceeding to Broken Hill. An African employee was helping me lift the heavy stretcher when he suddenly let go, shouting '*nyoka*' and I was left trying to cope with all the weight. After we eventually managed to get the stretcher into the compartment, the African was seen holding his foot and said he had been bitten by a *nyoka* (snake).

His foot began to swell visibly and, on shining a torch downwards, I saw a small snake in the vicinity which was dispatched forthwith. It was most likely a night adder, which dispelled the prevalent belief that snakes were never active at night. He was placed in the van of the train and we returned to Broken Hill with two patients, one more than anticipated.

On the south run we occasionally spent the night in Lusaka where, being the seat of government, much of the European population were civil servants. I went to the cinema there one Friday night. It was a warm night and, being early for the show, I stood talking to a colleague in the foyer — a government medical officer in full evening dress. The foyer began to fill with ladies and gentlemen, all in evening dress. When the performance was about to commence I suggested we went in, for I did not wish to miss the English news film usually shown at the beginning of each performance. To my amazement and amusement he said that as a matter of etiquette he could not enter the cinema before the governor. Eventually the governor arrived, about 15 minutes after the commencement of the programme, and was followed into the cinema by his retinue, about 60 civil servants and their wives, presumably in order of seniority. About three complete rows of the best seats were reserved for them and apparently this was a weekly routine. This custom of going to a cinema in Central Africa in evening dress on a warm night, awaiting the arrival of the governor and missing the best part of the programme, was a sad reflection of how idiotic the attitude of the British colonial administration could be at times.

Broken Hill mine, where lead, zinc and small quantities of vanadium and silver were mined, was named after the lead and zinc Broken Hill mine in Australia, the town taking the same name. It was run as a subsidiary company of Anglo-American, the vast mining group which owned gold, copper and other mines throughout southern and Central Africa. The general manager, a renowned metallurgist, and other senior mine staff were Americans, so Thanksgiving Day was a time of rejoicing for us all, with turkey and pumpkin pie as the traditional fare. The local cinema and a fine library had been provided by the mine. The general manager invited suggestions on what films to show and books to purchase, and most reasonable requests were met. Sumptuous dinners at the general manager's house, followed by attendance at a cinema show, was a routine Saturday night entertainment for some of us.

Apart from the African employees, the railwaymen stationed at Broken Hill were a mixed bag of Englishmen, South Africans, young Rhodesians and the odd foreigner. They were a tough crowd from a variety of social backgrounds. Some were former public school boys who had joined the railways after having failed as tobacco farmers in Rhodesia during the slump in the 1930s. One clerk was a recently demobilized naval lieutenant commander. Many were ex-railwaymen from the United Kingdom, but the majority were South Africans. When I first went to Broken Hill I was amused by the sight of a larger than average jovial engine driver who drove a shunting engine. His huge bulk oozed out of the side opening of the engine where he sat. He was obviously very popular among the other railwaymen because they all went out of their way to greet him. He was introduced to me as the leader of the Railway Workers' Union and his name was Roy Welensky. We eventually became friendly and I soon formed the opinion that he was an outstanding, charismatic individual. He was a born leader of men with a pleasant, commanding personality who certainly had 'the gift of the gab'. I discovered that he came from a humble background and was self-educated, but by the time I fist met him he was an aesthetic individual, fond of classical music and good literature. He had read most of the important biographies of world leaders and seemed to know all there was to know about Haley's classical *African Survey* on the British colonial empire. In addition to being a working engine driver and chairman of the Railway Workers' Union, he was a member of the Legislative Assembly of Northern Rhodesia and soon became its leader, the equivalent of the prime minister of an independent country. He was also made director of Manpower, a very important appointment during the war. For the same individual to be chairman of the Railway Workers' Union and director of Manpower, two diametrically opposed spheres of interest, shows how he was successfully able to run with the hares and hunt with the hounds. He was everything to every man, a born politician who had the ability to be a great

60

statesman and could have been, without exaggeration, a successful prime minister of the United Kingdom, or even president of the United States. As we became more friendly we visited each other's homes. Although he was born in Rhodesia and had never visited the United Kingdom, he was pro-British and not a racist. If political labels meant anything in Africa at that time, he could be described as a liberal. I often borrowed books from him and remember how enthusiastic he was about a book by Fenner Brockway, which revealed how Labour politicians were liquidated when they were patronized by Tory politicians or groups like the Astor set. In retrospect, it is a pity he did not heed the warning himself.

The Legislative Assembly in Northern Rhodesia was a body of persons consisting of heads of government departments, such as the director of medical services, and unofficial members drawn from the local community who were nominated by the governor or, in some instances, elected. They assisted and advised the governor in framing legislation. The governor was not bound to accept their advice and real power in the territory was directed from the Colonial Office in London through the governor. Roy Welensky was made its leader. The local unofficial member for Broken Hill was a typically upper-crust Englishman by the name of Gore Brown. He ran a large estate on the Great North Road where he farmed roses for the extraction of their essential perfume, which was very valuable and was sold to perfume manufacturers in Europe. He represented the special interests of Africans and the European railwaymen referred to him as 'Gore Black'.

Besides being his medical adviser, I was Roy Welensky's confidant and, because of the time interval, I can justifiably reveal some of the less contentious matters we discussed. The British government was well aware of his capabilities and popularity with all European workers and other settlers, no matter what political views they may have held. The governor and senior officials admired and respected him despite his humble background and trade union leadership. One day he telephoned me and said he urgently wished to discuss a cablegram he had received from the Colonial Office in London. It was signed by Andrew Cohen who was later knighted and became the governor of Uganda. In simple straightforward terms it offered him the full-time post of labour adviser to the Colonial Office in London at an attractive salary. My surmise was that the British government, aware of the influences he could use to exert pressure on it to grant independence or other demands for the benefit of the European residents, was offering him the post in order to get him out of the political limelight in Northern Rhodesia. My unhesitating advice to him was to accept the candidature offered by the British government in his own interest and that of his family. To be resident in London on a fat salary and to travel to all colonial territories at His Majesty's expense was too good an opportunity to be missed, despite any ulterior motive there may have been for the offer. His reply was that he intended to turn down the proposal because, in his own words, 'I hope to be the prime minister of Southern Rhodesia, Northern Rhodesia and Nyasaland.' In my ignorance I thought he had become a megalomaniac, but, as he explained, Sir Godfrey Huggins, the then prime minister of Southern Rhodesia, 'will make the idea of a Federation of Central Africa public in the near future and you watch them all fall for it'. My reply was simply to state that I did not think that a federation of the two Rhodesias and Nyasaland was possible now or in the future. Once again, how wrong I was.

I do not recollect much about the African population in Northern Rhodesia or Broken Hill in particular at this time. As stated before, they appeared to be a docile, happy people, hard working and contented. Educated Africans were few and far between. To my surprise, an African government employee came to see me for a medical life insurance examination on behalf of a South African insurance company. To fill in the section on his home conditions I had to make a special visit to the African township or 'location' where all Africans lived. To my surprise, his standard of living was as high as that of the average European settler. Minor episodes like this made me aware of change in Africa and I consequently began to think about the future.

As in Southern Rhodesia, a rigid colour bar operated. Although there were no apartheid laws, as in South Africa, the races rarely mixed socially. Skilled jobs on the mines and railways were reserved for Europeans. All drivers, firemen, shunters, guards, fitters and other artisans, and even dining-car waiters, were Europeans and their trade unions selfishly protected their interests. As passengers on the railway, Africans travelled in hard third- or fourth-class compartments and, even if they had a first-class ticket, they were barred from making use of the dining car.

Some time in 1944 the chief railway medical officer, stationed at Bulawayo, made his annual tour of the railway system. I was responsible for running a European clinic in the railway camp and an African clinic in the railways' African township. As was usual, the official in charge of the African township was a European. We were inspecting the township when the chief medical officer noted that nearly all the little homesteads had large numbers of bags of maize stored in odd places. The official in charge suggested that the reason for this was the unusually good crop harvested that year and his explanation was accepted by us. A few months later a most unpredictable event occurred. At exactly 8.00 a.m. one morning all the African railway employees stopped working, no matter what task they were performing. Goods were left partially unloaded from trucks and many jobs were left uncompleted. With a smile and respectful farewell to their European supervisors they returned to their homes in the railway township or compound. They were on strike for improved pay and conditions. The reason for the supplies of maize in their homes now became apparent, but their action had not even been anticipated by the police special branch.

I had been told about previous labour troubles on the Copper-belt resulting in the slaughter of the strikers and also about recent labour troubles in Bulawayo, but this sudden unexpected strike in Broken Hill came as shock to us all. The European employees became very concerned and emotional about the episode. One railwayman actually called at my residence during the crisis and requested me to attend a special meeting at the Railway Club the next evening called by the European Workers' Union to consider the matter. European employees managed to keep some trains running but many had to be cancelled. My medical orderly, after negotiations with the strike leaders, was allowed to keep on working, but I was instructed not to enter the African compound.

Routine African clinics were cancelled because of the strike and it may be of interest to digress and explain the attitudes of Africans in Central Africa to European medical practice. Although we saw many patients the proportion of those we saw requiring and seeking medical advice was comparatively small. Most likely we only scratched the surface and attended to 'the tip of the iceberg'. It is safe to assume that a large proportion of our African patients only consulted us because their own *nganga* (witch doctor) had failed to treat them successfully. Their attitude to disease was fatalistic and they did not cherish the idea of going into hospital because it was a place where people died. If one successfully carried out a new type of operation such as the removal of a large thyroid gland it was usual to be inundated with a large number of patients with a similar complaint all requesting surgical treatment. As a rule there was simply no time available to carry out these long, time-consuming operations on large numbers of patients.

There were two types of *nganga*. The evil better-known variety who dressed up in animal skins, threw bones and diagnosed disease as being due to evil spirits or individuals; the latter were murdered on occasions because of their suspected evil influence. The majority of *nganga*s were not evil but diagnosed and treated disease with native medicines obtained from roots, plants and parts of animals. I often referred patients, especially those with psychological problems, to *nganga*s who obtained better results that we did practising modern European medicine.

To return to the strike. I attended the European Workers' Union meeting, inconspicuously sitting in the back row, and was horrified by the anti-black sentiment and feeling shown by the European workers. I was sorry to see that the meeting was addressed by Roy Welensky, who sensed the prevalent attitudes and made an anti-black speech, quite out of keeping with his true sentiments, which I knew intimately. Welensky's cookboy had assaulted one of his wives with a stick for alleged disloyalty. I treated the lady concerned and was therefore conversant with the facts. Welensky insinuated that Africans were now becoming violent and related this episode at the meeting, giving a completely wrong impression of the personal nature of the assault. Events and life, even in Africa, could be frustrating at times and this was an instance of the European railway workers' mindless hatred and intolerance making it impossible for them to realize or even consider that the

African employees were fellow workers seeking to improve their miserable pay and conditions. Blind racism overcame any reasonable sense of fairness. The strike ended after a couple of weeks when the railway management promised to set up a special arbitration inquiry to consider their wage claims.

As a result of the strike, which showed that the developing Africans were capable of organized protest, a special arbitration was set up and held at Broken Hill within the next couple of months. I had no official interest in the inquiry but became fully involved because the general manager of the Rhodesia Railways, a very important individual in those days, stayed at our home for about a week during the period of the inquiry, which consisted of a one-man arbitrator, a lawyer who had recently been leader of the Opposition in the South African Parliament. The latter stayed with the provincial commissioner and this led to social complications, more upsetting for my wife than myself. We were not invited to a banquet given for the important individuals attending the tribunal at the provincial commissioner's residence — we were *personae non gratae* — and we did not invite the provincial commissioner to a party given at our house. The general manager and others were amused when I had to explain the reasons for the reciprocal omissions and consequent transport problems and felt confident that they were all on our side as far as the contretemps was concerned. The lawyer who came up from Bulawayo to present the African workers' case, and who later became a judge in Rhodesia, stayed at the local hotel and was rather left out in the cold.

It does not surprise me when one reads in the press these days that workers' unions refuse to go before an arbitration inquiry to adjudicate on their demands. I would not reveal any details but suffice to say that I knew the result of this particular inquiry many days before it was published or, indeed, had even been completed. An interesting aspect of the inquiry was that the Africans who represented the workers and gave evidence were very unsophisticated. Surprisingly one was a sweeper who daily came to clean the drains in our garden, but as the years went by I was to become accustomed to this unexpected whim of African leadership.

Life and events continued to be interesting and adventurous during the next couple of years in Broken Hill which was, after all, only a clearing in the bush and one's social life depended on pleasant human relations. Societies such as the Women's Institute flourished and the Sons of England was very active and ardently supported by those who considered themselves to be the true representatives of the good old bulldog breed. A couple of fanatical Scottish nationalists had large flags with the lion rampant flying from their residential roof tops. This illustrates a well-known fact that individuals tend to become more nationalistic the further away they are from their country of origin. Anniversaries such as Burns Nicht, St George's Day and even Thanksgiving Day were great occasions for Europeans in the town and were celebrated with exaggerated fervour.

Most of the leading settlers were Freemasons and in an indirect way I was personally advised to be 'on the square' for my own good. Roy Welensky's wife, a fine, independent-minded, forthright individual of Afrikaans extraction, told me of how her husband had kept their family poor to the extent of being short of food and clothes on one occasion because he had to invest his month's wages in an evening dress outfit for his Freemason banquets, or whatever their gatherings are called.

The district or senior railway engineer was an erudite individual who had previously been a university lecturer in mathematics and successfully avoided the restrictions of married life because his family lived in South Africa while he spent his time inspecting the railway line in a motor trolley, a converted car which ran on rails. He was a renegade Freemason who was quite willing to give away their secret signs since he had abandoned their futilities. He told hair-raising stories of how he had been involved in suppressing criminal responsibility when helping fellow Freemasons. In the course of time I personally experienced the distress sign of Freemasons and noted how they supported their fellow secret society adherents to the detriment of non-followers of the creed.

The Ossewabrandwag was an Afrikaans so-called cultural secret society which was founded in South Africa in 1938 to perpetuate the inspiration of the Great Trek in that country. In fact it was an extreme right-wing organization which was anti-British and pro-German. At this time it had the support of most Afrikaners who desired to make South Africa a republic. They thought that

Germany was winning the war and were rejoicing prematurely because they imagined republican status would be granted to them when an armistice was declared.

The local leader of the society, a railway guard, had his legs severed under a railway truck while attempting to replace a broken coupling with a temporary drawbar. The accident occurred about halfway between Broken Hill and Ndola. When the driver and fireman came back to see what had happened and saw him lying under the truck with both his legs crushed, they must have panicked because they uncoupled the engine and drove it to the next siding ahead to phone for help. It was ironic that the African coalboy who assisted the European fireman stayed to help and comfort the injured man in his predicament. The accident occurred in the small hours of the morning and I went to the scene of the incident, which was virtually miles from anywhere, in the engineer's motor trolley. Because of his severe injuries we were unable to move the patient on the stretcher into the small trolley. We slung an emergency telephone cable onto the telegraph wires alongside the track and requested Kpiri Mposhi to arrange for the clearance of the line and bring the mixed mail train, held up at a siding further north, through as quickly as possible to pick us up and proceed to Broken Hill.

In the meantime I was left on my own with the patient who, despite an injection of morphia, was semi-conscious and in pain. I decided to give him a slow drip anaesthetic where he lay on the stretcher. We had not been there long before I could hear a rustling noise in the bush and, soon after, the roar of a lion, which sounded much too close for comfort. The thought entered my head that with the smell of blood around it may attract the lion or lions and that it did not make logical sense that both of us should be devoured. I pulled the stretcher to the base of the telegraph pole and climbed up and down again as a trial manoeuvre. For some reason I did not panic but got through to Kpiri Mposhi on the emergency telephone, explained my predicament and requested them to hurry up the train. It was a relief to hear the station foreman's voice coolly advise me not to worry and to make a fire which would keep the lion or lions away. Fortunately the connection between cigarette smoking and cancer of the lung was not to be noted for another ten years, so matches were available. I was scared to go too far to gather wood but managed to start a small fire with dry grass and small twigs, gradually becoming more adventuresome and collecting larger pieces of dry wood to add to the flames. It was a great relief when the mail train eventually picked us up and it was 10.00 a.m. by the time we arrived back in Broken Hill where I had to perform a double amputation. The poor chap died a few days later.

Accidents similar to the one described were not rare events during the years I served as a railway medical officer. On one occasion I received an urgent message in the middle of the night that a ganger's wife stationed about 30 miles south of Broken Hill had unexpectedly gone into labour. There was no road to the cottage and there were no northbound trains passing there for some hours. The southbound mail train was scheduled to leave Broken Hill in about five minutes. I delayed its departure, rushed down to the station and, after requesting the driver to proceed as fast as possible, we set off at 3.10 a.m. I sat in the guard's van with the guard. When the train stopped at the cottage I jumped off, but in the dark could not see a thing. The guard explained that the cottage was a short walk back and the driver had stopped further along because he would not be able to get the train started again if he had stopped directly outside the cottage, which was on a curved incline. He showed his green light and the train quickly disappeared into the darkness.

I stumbled back along the track but when I heard a rustling in the bush started to run. Eventually I saw the cottage but there was a deep ditch between it and the track. I could not see the small footbridge and clamoured through the ditch coming out with a soaking wet lower part and covered with mud. I charged up the garden path and without knocking rushed through the front door. A surprised ganger, with the ubiquitous hurricane lamp in his hand, took me to the bedroom where his wife lay smiling in bed with a contented newborn baby in the crib alongside. The ganger, in all seriousness, explained that he found his wife easy because he had delivered many cows in the past! The baby had been washed and dressed, and he had even given it a dessertspoon full of castor oil before my arrival. Despite the medication both mother and child did well.

One day my son, then aged about one year, became unusually restless and began to cry in the early hours of the morning. I went to his room, which was in a suite across the passage from ours, to find out the cause of his restlessness; I was aghast to see a mass of black army ants crawling over his mosquito net, which appeared to be black rather than its normal white colour. Very few ants had been able to penetrate the net because of its small mesh, which may possibly have saved him from serious consequences. I disconnected the net from its hooks, grabbed him from his bed and carried him to safety. It was noted that the ants had gained entry through the bath outlet pipe in the adjacent bathroom; the pipe discharged into a small outside drain. A bucketful of wood ash from the boiler was immediately sprinkled over the room to prevent the ants from progressing further into the house. These large ants were called army or soldier ants because they advanced in columns similar to an army on the march, clearing all in their path, devouring large insects or small animals before them. I had heard of cases of African babies who had died following an attack by these ants and we felt relieved that the mosquito net and my son's warning cry had saved him from his dangerous predicament. The perimeter of our residence was henceforth surrounded by a sprinkling of wood ash. For some reason, the creatures did not march through wood ash.

During the time I worked there, Broken Hill European Hospital was a small inadequate building which had previously been the mine club. The operating theatre had been the billiard room and marks on the floor showed where the billiard table had once stood. However, with a dedicated nursing staff we managed to cope with all emergencies and had comparatively good results.

On one occasion a Dakota aircraft full of South African troops flying home from the north crashed in flames in the bush about 20 miles from the town. Many were killed and others severely injured and burned. I spent 12 hours in the operating theatre without a break dealing with the severely injured. The St John's Ambulance men called in to assist the nursing staff went out to be physically sick and then returned to help once again. I admired their tenacity.

The African hospital, also a mine property, was a series of corrugated iron hutments. During the rainy season, which has tropical downpours, lightning, thunder and torrents of rain that have to be experienced to be believed, I was operating on an African patient with a strangulated hernia — a condition for which an emergency operation has to be carried out to release the strangulation and so relieve the bowel blockage that would be fatal if not dealt with in a hurry. With part of the patient's bowel in my hands the lights were struck by lightning and we were left in pitch black darkness. With the aid of hurricane lamps and a torch I was completing the operation and was about to return the now unstrangulated bowel to the abdominal cavity when the storm abated, but as we were the only lighted room in the area it became filled with flying ants, which invariably come out of the ground at the end of a storm. It became a hopeless procedure trying to remove the ants from my own eyes, hands and, indeed, the patient's bowel lying on the operating table. In trepidation, for the operating procedure was no longer sterile and bits of flying ant had certainly gained entry to the abdominal cavity, I eventually managed to return the bowel and stitch up the wound. Although antibiotics were not yet available the patient, however, made an uninterrupted recovery.

Momentous events were happening in Europe. The Allies had landed in Normandy, buzz bombs were landed on England and important days came and were forgotten. Parochial life in Broken Hill went on undisturbed. A large well-known transport firm in the town had the monopoly to transport goods by road from Broken Hill, the railhead, to various parts of the territory and further afield to adjacent countries such as Tanganyika. All its drivers were European and towards the end of the war they were called up for military service. There was no alternative but to replace them with Africans.

This calamity, which was sure to result in the ruination of the firm and its owners because of untrustworthy black employees, was the main topic of conversation. The result was completely different from the pessimistic outlook. The Africans turned out to be careful drivers who caused less damage to their heavy-duty motor vehicles than their white counterparts and were more reliable in their schedules, especially because they consumed less alcohol. So much for the discussions we had had in Bulawayo a few years previously when pundits had expressed their opinions on how many decades it would take before Africans could be entrusted to perform any job requiring mechanical knowledge or a minimum of initiative.

Crime was almost unknown and the local police force did not have much to do. Houses were not locked at night and shoppers would leave parcels in cars parked at the curbside with their windows open. Keys were invariably left in the ignition. I can recollect only one case of burglary or petty thieving ever being reported. This was when the visiting son of a retired naval officer broke into a local store and stole a quantity of watches; these were subsequently recovered when he attempted to sell them in a bar in Bulawayo a few days later.

I was rapidly gaining experience in the art of my profession, not only the practical aspects such as delivering babies or the removal of an appendix, but more important, aspects of human nature one never suspected during the years spent as a student or working in hospitals. If you were to ask the average white South African or Rhodesian what he thought of novels with an African background, such as Alan Paton's *Too Late the Phalarope* or Doris Lessing's *The Grass is Singing*, the invariable reply would be that they were 'too far fetched' and that relationships between the races simply did not occur as portrayed in these stories. I can assure you they would be wrong. On two occasions I called unexpectedly at the homes of female patients because I happened to be in the vicinity and caught them in bed with their African servants and — even more unbelievable — they were both Afrikaans married women.

I was once called to attend to a battered wife. It is unnecessary to explain her condition in detail but I was shocked to see how on one occasion she had been so severely battered that both her eyes were black and closed, her lips split open and she had terrible weals on her body. She was a distressing sight and, because of my inexperience, I lost no time in informing the police. Her husband was charged in the local magistrates' court and I was called upon to give evidence. In court both spouses treated me as a hostile witness and made out that I was making 'a mountain out of a molehill' and that they were both very much in love with each other. This was the first time I had become involved with masochists and, as far as possible, I was careful to keep out of marital squabbles in the future. I also encountered a nymphomaniac, a young married buxom wench who requested a visit. When I felt myself being pulled into the bed I rapidly terminated the examination and hurriedly made my exodus.

Shortly after the thrice weekly arrival of the mail train from the south to Ndola, the Congo mail train for Elizabethville left there for the north. A through passenger coach was provided from Bulawayo so that it was possible to travel from Cape Town to Elizabethville with only one change at Bulawayo. The Congo railway employees were practically all Africans, only supervisors, inspectors, and certain skilled workers were Belgian Europeans. The Rhodesia Railways Workers' Union objected to an African engine driver working in Rhodesia so that a European inspector drove the engine from the Congo border to Ndola, eight miles in distance, and also on its return trip. A favourite sight was to stand beyond the end of the platform at Ndola and watch the inspector hand over the controls to the black driver, hop off the engine and on to the dining car before the train gathered speed. In practice, the European was at the controls when the train left the station and this apparently satisfied the pride of the Rhodesia Railway European workers. This was another instance of how idiotic the colour bar could be in Central Africa.

I had a Belgian businessman, resident in the Congo, as a patient. He forcibly expressed the opinion that the British were incompetent colonists who did not give the indigenous population an opportunity to develop and cited the example of the railways where, in the Congo, practically all railwaymen were Africans, whereas in the Rhodesias blacks were only allowed to perform unskilled labouring and menial jobs. He thought there would be economic and political chaos in British Central Africa in a relatively short time because of their short-sighted policy, whereas the Congo would flourish because of the more liberal attitude adopted towards the economic development of the indigenous population. Of course, we were soon to know how wrong his prognostications were. At this time India was granted her independence. The local Indian community gave a sumptuous dinner in the town public gardens to celebrate the occasion. Most of the leading European residents were invited and Africans were conspicuous by their absence, as were some of the Europeans who, unwilling to celebrate the break-up of the British Empire, found some convenient reason to be out of town.

We were stationed in Broken Hill for about four years. In 1947 I was offered a transfer to Livingstone, near the Victoria Falls. The offer was readily accepted. In the meantime, Welensky in Northern Rhodesia and Huggins, the prime minister of Southern Rhodesia, commenced their advocacy of a closer union between the two Rhodesias and suggested they should be amalgamated for their common interest. In the latter part of the year, my family and I occupied a compartment in the mixed mail train bound for Livingstone. Our pets were accommodated in the dog cage in the goods van. A large covered goods truck contained our belongings and another truck our car. We were sorry to leave Broken Hill, where we had had a happy social life and I had had a satisfying and interesting professional occupation, but were keen to settle in Livingstone, which was less isolated in the wilds of Central Africa.

4

Livingstone and the Central African Federation

L ivingstone, which is situated seven miles from the Victoria Falls on the Zambezi River, was a far more sophisticated town than Broken Hill. In addition to being the shopping centre for the numerous tourists who visited the Victoria Falls, the Northern Rhodesian government departments, including the Department of Justice presided over by the chief justice, were stationed there. It had recently been made a new railway district with a large increase in administrative staff and a large international airport was under construction in the vicinity. The Flying Boat Service from the United Kingdom to South Africa commenced within days of our arrival. The flying boats landed on the Zambezi River about four miles upstream of the falls. A reception building had been constructed on the south bank of the river where the boats landed. I was appointed local BOAC medical officer to attend to their local staff and to any passenger or flying staff in need of medical attention. The flying boat from the north landed on three afternoons each week.

The famous Victoria Falls Hotel, in close proximity to the falls, was also situated on the south bank of the river. It was owned and run by the Rhodesia Railways and was reputed to be among the five leading hotels in the world, taking into consideration its siting, service, facilities and food. At that time the majority of visitors to the hotel travelled there by train. The railway station was situated in the picturesque hotel garden. As a railway official, full facilities,

which included tennis, swimming, cabaret dancing and other entertainments, were available to us at the Victoria Falls Hotel, to
which visitors came from all parts of the world.

My professional life was extremely busy and varied; I had also
been appointed to the post of Southern Rhodesia government
medical officer. I ran a clinic at the hotel for European visitors and
staff, as well as an African clinic in the village compound on three
afternoons each week. My patients ranged from royalty at the
Victoria Falls Hotel to Bushmen. Mine was the nearest African
clinic to northern Bechuanaland, where many nomadic Bushmen
roamed, living off the countryside they shared with the wild
animals. The occasional Bushman we saw at the clinic was easily
recognizable by the light brown colour of his skin, small stature
and large buttocks. The top of their buttocks were shelved to the
extent that small objects could be balanced on the protrusion.

My first duty when visiting the south bank of the river was to
meet the southbound flying boat on behalf of the government. The
base was classified as an international sanitary airport. The crew
and passengers would have spent the previous night at Entebbe in
Uganda on the shores of Lake Victoria. It was a yellow-fever area
and it was our responsibility to prevent the spread of the disease,
which is carried by mosquitoes, or any other infectious disease,
into Rhodesia.

The customs and immigration officers, my African assistant and
I would go out onto the river in a large motorboat to meet the
craft. As the flying boat landed it was my duty to enquire from the
captain if there were any sick persons on board.

My assistant would spray the entrance with insecticide before we
entered the craft. He would then continue to spray the whole
interior of the craft in order to kill off any mosquitoes that may
have entered it in Uganda. They were not the same type of
mosquito that carried the malaria parasite.

While this was going on I would go upstairs to the bar and buy
as many miniature bottles of whisky as my pockets would
accommodate without looking obvious. I would also buy tins of
30 Players cigarettes, which easily slipped into my side pockets.
Whisky was almost unobtainable in Livingstone and this happy
arrangement ensured an adequate supply of whisky and imported

cigarettes for our guests and ourselves. The customs officer often told me that he would 'discover a smuggler one of these days'.

There was an immigration and customs barrier on the road to Livingstone about a mile away from the falls and a similar barrier about the same distance from the falls on the south bank. There was a police station and customs post alongside this barrier. The area between these two barriers, which included the famous railway and road bridge over the gorge below the falls, could be described as neutral territory. As the Southern Rhodesia government medical officer, I automatically became the local police surgeon and commissioner of oaths. Special permission was granted for me to practise in both Northern and Southern Rhodesia. I called at the police station each time I visited Victoria Falls to examine any prisoners or policemen and their families who required medical attention. The personnel stationed at the police post consisted of a sergeant in charge, a trooper, a member of the Criminal Investigation Department (who also acted as an immigration officer) and 12 African constables. They were members of the British South Africa Police. As mentioned before, they were a fine disciplined body of men. Their incredible sense of duty and discipline was exemplified by the attitude of the sergeant in charge when his commanding officer phoned him from Bulawayo. On answering the call, he immediately sat to attention and replied respectfully with frequent interjections of 'no sir' and 'yes sir'; I witnessed this remarkable exhibition on a number of occasions. Most of my police work consisted of requests to prepare medico-legal postmortem reports in cases of sudden death, or when foul play was suspected. I have often asked my colleagues in England, who had not worked abroad or in circumstances in which they were the sole medical practitioner attending to a large population, what they would consider to be the most difficult and worrying part of their practice. Most thought that it was the carrying out of difficult emergency operations, blocked labour, or conditions requiring a consultant's opinion. As far as I was concerned the problem that worried me most was being unable to be sure of the cause of death after completing a detailed medico-legal postmortem examination. Presiding judges or magistrates usually made it very clear that they were not pleased to accept an uncertain cause of death in these cases. It is a long time ago now, so I do not mind admitting that I bluffed numerous police officers by pointing out blocked coronary arteries with a probe during a postmortem examination when I was not at all sure that the artery concerned was in any way abnormal! When I admitted this lapse of honesty to a senior colonial medical officer, his immediate reply was that he had often been in the same predicament. This reply helped to assuage my guilty conscience.

When I first arrived at Victoria Falls, police patrols were carried out on horseback, but latterly a police Land-Rover and motorcycles were used. The trooper would drive the cycle and the African constable would sit on the back seat of the vehicle, in close proximity to the trooper and holding onto his waist. It was difficult to imagine a closer example of partnership between the races! One often became involved in cases of assault, rape, manslaughter and even murder. The police, who were responsible for law and order in a very large area, depended on paid informers who rarely failed to keep them informed of any unusual incident or lawbreaking in remote areas of their district.

An event that stands out in my memory was an incident in which a human skeleton was found deep in a woodland area many miles from the police station. A trooper, an African constable and I travelled as far as we could in a Land-Rover and then had to walk miles to the site of the incident. On the way we came upon a clearing in the forest. There were a few mud and grass huts in the clearing, but what was more unusual was the sight of about 20 men sitting in a semicircle drinking beer. Up to that time it was usual for Africans to have the utmost respect for Europeans and to treat a European constable with awe — the BSAP had by now replaced its army ranks with the usual police titles. On this occasion they chose to ignore us completely and pretend we were not there. On an enquiry by the African constable, one individual pointed in the direction of the incident and no word was spoken. The European constable lost his cool and began to shout at the silent congregation. I personally felt a sense of incredulity and fear and requested him not to interfere with them because we were hopelessly outnumbered. This episode was a sign of the times — the 'wind of change' was beginning to blow in Central Africa. I was later informed that a large number of Africans had been trans-ferred from urban areas in Southern Rhodesia and given land in remote areas on grounds of security. In fact, on the advice of the police and army, security against African insurrection was the main consideration in the siting of all new native townships, or settlements, in Southern Rhodesia.

An enterprising new pilot, who owned a single-engined, light, six-seater aircraft, started up an air service to enable visitors to view the falls from the air and to observe wild game. On a visit to the Victoria Falls Hotel one afternoon, the clerk at the hotel foyer who booked his prospective clients, inquired whether I had seen Terrence, the young pilot. He had apparently taken visitors on a flight early that morning, but had not been seen since. I had not seen him, but the next day discovered that the five visitors who had booked to go on his flight the previous day had not appeared at meals and had not used their rooms that night. It was presumed that the plane had landed in a remote location or had crashed.

The government instituted a wide and thorough air reconnais-sance search, but after a few days, when no aircraft or wreckage were observed from the air, no communication was received from the pilot or passengers and no tribesman had reported seeing a crashed aircraft, it was presumed the plane had crashed into the river or thick bush. About a month later, a farmer who ran a dairy farm about 15 miles upriver on the south bank reported to the police that one of his African herdsmen had found the wreckage of an aircraft and human remains scattered around in the vicinity, in thick woodland, a few miles from his farm in the direction of the falls. Apparently the discovery was made because the cattle began to bellow in a loud and unusual manner, which they usually do when they notice anything unfamiliar in their surroundings.

The sergeant in charge of the police post, an African constable, and I set out in the police Land-Rover to locate and report on the incident. We eventually found the site, with great difficulty, deep in the woodland area, which was thick with tall indigenous trees. Four large white sheets were spread out over the treetops to guide the original air searchers to the site. They eventually reported that the wrecked aircraft under the trees was invisible from the air. The human remains had been dragged about and devoured by scavenging animals and birds, leaving bare skeletons. At a later date we were given to understand that complications arose because the unfortunate individuals involved in the crash did not turn out to be husbands and wives as recorded in the hotel register! In those days before the advent of common-law husbands and wives, couples visiting the Victoria Falls Hotel were in trouble if one of them had to be admitted to hospital and had to confess that they were unmarried. The oldest couple I encountered in this predicament were both aged over 75 years.

While on the subject of policing, one evening a police truck arrived at our residence in Livingstone. The sergeant in charge of the Victoria Falls police post, who had been driving the truck, was invited in for a sundowner, which he readily accepted. While he was on his second drink, my wife became concerned about an objectionable smell on the veranda and started to look around for its source. Suddenly our guest remembered the reason for his visit. He wanted me to conduct a postmortem on a decomposed body in his police truck alongside our veranda. The source of the objectionable odour became obvious!

A magistrate would come up to the Victoria Falls police post once a fortnight and I would invariably be called upon to give medical evidence in relevant cases. The law and court procedures in Southern Rhodesia, where Roman Dutch law was practised, were different from those in Northern Rhodesia, where English law was used. One had to be careful to remember in which territory the evidence was being given. A black person in Southern Rhodesia was officially referred to as a native. In Northern Rhodesia, where the name native would be regarded as pejorative, he was called an African. It was a crime to attempt to commit suicide in Northern Rhodesia, but not in Southern Rhodesia. Written evidence, for example a postmortem report, could be handed in to the court in Livingstone, but not at Victoria Falls, where the report had to be read out in court. A proportion of criminal cases were referred to the High Court when the accused was brought before a judge and jury. This necessitated my travelling to Bulawayo about once every three months for the quarterly sessions. At times I was called upon to appear as a medical witness in the magistrates' court, or even High Court, in Livingstone. The local judge was an outstanding individual who had previously been the chief prosecutor at the Nuremberg trials in Germany. He conducted his court with outstanding refinement and solemnity. The police in Livingstone were colonial police; most of the Europeans amongst them had served in the Palestine police force before the establishment of Israel.

Their attitude towards the African population was more liberal and relaxed than that of the BSAP. They called me out on one occasion to see one of my patients at her home in Livingstone because, as they put it, she was 'acting in a peculiar manner'. On arrival at her home I was surprised to see the woman concerned, a German refugee, chasing two policemen round and round the dining-room table brandishing a carving knife. They immediately informed me that they were going to obtain a magistrate's order to have her certified and requested me to take over. She eventually calmed down and was admitted to hospital from where she absconded the next day and took a bus to the Victoria Falls. Once there, she coolly approached a visitor, who had recently been discharged from the army, asked him to hold her coat and handbag, which he took and, to his horror, jumped over the edge into the Eastern Cataract. She was never seen again. On my arrival at the scene the visitor was visibly shaken and required the administration of a sedative.

One night, while walking from one part of our house to the other I noticed a door leading from a bedroom to the veranda move. It occurred to me that it was not possible for the door to move on its own on such a still evening and went to investigate. On looking out of the door, I saw an African standing against the wall with a bundle under his arm. As soon as he saw me he dropped the bundle and made off into the garden through an exit door from the gauzed veranda. I chased him and managed to bring him down on the lawn, where we fought each other ferociously. I kept shouting 'help! help!' without any response. It was like a bad dream. I luckily managed to kick him in a vulnerable part of his anatomy, which was most painful, and he lay down with me sitting on top of him. My wife eventually arrived and enquired if I had caught a snake. 'Yes,' I replied, 'a big black one and send for the police immediately.' They came and took him away. A few minutes later I received a call from the African hospital requesting me to attend a patient who had been assaulted by a European in the railway area. Following my explanation, the government medical officer was called to attend to him. The blankets on our beds and all my wearing apparel had been removed from my cupboard. I had caught him on his third visit to our home and all our possessions were found in a ditch a short distance away. He made an uneventful recovery and was sentenced to two years' hard labour.

When visiting Victoria Falls on three afternoons each week it was my custom to park in the car park on the Northern Rhodesian side of the falls to await the sight of the flying boat overhead. If I then crossed the bridge and drove to the base, my arrival would coincide with our going out to meet the aircraft. A troupe of baboons habitually lived in the bush adjoining the car park. It was interesting to observe their family life, which was close to that of human beings. A large male baboon, the undisputed leader of the troupe, received universal respect from all the other male and female baboons, who would immediately carry out his commands. I once saw a baby baboon fall off its mother's back when crossing the adjacent road and being killed by a passing car. The abject misery of the mother who picked up and attempted to revive her dead infant was touching to observe. On one hot afternoon, when there were few visitors to the falls, a large American car drove up and parked nearby. The European driver got out of the vehicle, the back of which was loaded with cardboard boxes, in order to view the falls. He had left one of the windows partially open and, as soon as he had gone, I saw a baboon put its arm through the gap, unwind the window and enter the car. The car must have been owned by a commercial traveller because, within a short while, a number of the troupe had got into it and opened the boxes which contained ladies' underwear. It was amusing to see baboons running around with bras around their necks and ladies' pants pulled up their arms.

Wild animals were plentiful in the falls area, which included the Wankie Game Reserve. Curiously enough, more wildlife was observed in the surrounding country than in the reserve itself. On the few occasions we visited the reserve to view animals, we were disappointed at how few we saw.

Elephant were often observed on both banks of the river above the falls. One young European visitor hurled a stone at an elephant, which responded by picking him up with its trunk and crushing him to death underfoot. On two occasions I was required to perform postmortems on Africans who had been mauled by crocodiles. Monkey bites requiring medical attention were not infrequent.

Another troupe of baboons lived in the bush near the front of the hotel and visitors having their afternoon tea on the veranda would be surprised by baboons coming up to snatch cakes from their tables. Africans were specially employed to keep the baboons and monkeys away from the hotel by brandishing large poles to beat them off. In fact 'baboon operative' was an officially-designated grade of worker in the railways. Because the baboons had a habit of hurling rocks at trains passing through the cuttings between the falls and Wankie, baboon 'boys' were employed every day of the year to keep these animals away from the tops of the cuttings.

Visitors to a small game park in Livingstone would frequently, despite the warning signs, put their hands out of car windows to stroke a zebra. A severely-bitten hand was the usual result. Hippopotami could often be seen on a section of the road between Livingstone and Victoria Falls that passed close to the river. Packs of wild dogs, said to be the most vicious of all wild animals, could also be seen, as could wild boar and numerous species of small and large antelope or, as they were called, 'buck'. On one occasion we were motoring south on holiday when, early in the morning, about 20 miles from Livingstone, we were completely surrounded by what we thought were domestic animals until my young son noticed they were wild buffalo, which had a reputation of turning nasty. We spent an uncomfortable 20 minutes sitting quietly in the car until they dispersed.

When predatory baboons and Vandalic elephants became too plentiful in the falls area, it became the duty of the local game ranger to reduce their numbers by shooting. It was always a great windfall for the Africans who came from miles around to help themselves to the elephant meat, which they considered a delicacy — especially the trunk. It was quite an experience to see them hacking away at the huge carcasses with pickaxes and covered with blood from head to toe. The women would gather as much meat as they were able to carry on their heads for the seven-mile journey from Victoria Falls back to their homes in Livingstone. As they walked along the side of the road, the blood trickling off the meat would run down their backs and thereby blaze a bloody trail — it was an amazing sight. The game warden had difficulty carrying out his task of culling the baboons. As soon as they saw him with a gun they disappeared into the bush at such speed that he was unable to get a shot at them. He eventually managed to complete his invidious duty by dressing up as a female and concealing his firearm in the voluminous clothing. Baboons apparently do not expect a lady to be capable of such abhorrent behaviour and nor did they appreciate the practice of transvestism!

Snakes were numerous. I was once giving an intravenous injection to an African patient in the Livingstone clinic when, to my consternation, a snake crawled through a hole in the floor between the patient and myself. The syringe went flying as we hurriedly moved out of the way. It is interesting to note that in all my years of active medical practice in Africa I did not see a single fatal case of snakebite. Broadly speaking, there are two types of poisonous snakes, the *Elapidae* or cobra family and the *Viperidae*. The cobra, which has a hollow fang through which the venom is injected when it bites, is by far the most poisonous. Black and green mambas were often seen by us when walking in the bush. They move at a rapid speed and it is said they are able to keep up with a galloping horse. Whenever we encountered them in the bush they crossed our path at such speed that they could only be seen as a vanishing black or green streak and a quiver in the adjacent grass. When a mamba was experimentally put into a cage with a sheep, the unfortunate animal died within minutes of being bitten, for the venom contains a nerve poison. Farmers have told me of their livestock occasionally dying from snakebite after walking under a tree. My personal experience has been that most snakes of the cobra family rapidly get out of the way of approaching human beings.

The puff adder is the most common type of viper in Central Africa. Because puff adders are sluggish and slow moving, we saw them fairly frequently on our walks through the bush. Their fangs are grooved for the delivery of venom and they often cling to their victims. Numerous cases of snakebite were treated at the local hospital and almost invariably they had a swollen and infected foot. Africans who trod on a sluggish adder while walking barefoot in the bush would receive the bite in that part of their anatomy. It is interesting to note that adder venom causes clotting of blood cells. When I was a medical student in London, a young patient with haemophilia, a condition in which the blood lacks the essential clotting factor, was suffering from a persistent bleeding tooth socket following a tooth extraction and was being kept alive with blood transfusions. Some bright medical enthusiast thought of treating the condition with the venom of the Russell's viper — a snake commonly found in North America — and a supply was requested from America. The substance was rushed across the Atlantic on the *Queen Mary* liner and placed in the tooth socket. The bleeding stopped. The next day, a call was received from America advising us that they had sent us the wrong venom (it had been inactivated by heat) and that the active therapeutic substance was on its way to England.

This form of treatment was eventually found to be ineffective in the treatment of haemophiliacs, but as a young student it taught me a useful lesson. This was that each disease follows its own natural course. It will either cure itself or prove fatal, irrespective of the treatment. As a practitioner in later life I became aware that, however serious a patient's illness, there was always a chance that it would temporarily or permanently cure itself. Hence the assertion by an unknown wag that, 'The practice of medicine may be described as the art or science of amusing a sick man with frivolous speculation about his disease until such time that nature doth either kill or cure.'

During our stay in Africa we had a number of encounters with snakes. After seeing us off in the car to the local cinema in Livingstone one night, our European nurse came across one in our small toilet. She had already pulled her pants down before she realized she was sharing it with a four-foot-long snake. She yelled to our African servants for help and the cook rapidly dispatched the offending reptile, but I do not, however, consider it had been poisonous. On another occasion I was requested to accompany the

Broken Hill railway station, Northern Rhodesia (Zambia)

The author's wife

The author

Sir Roy Welensky

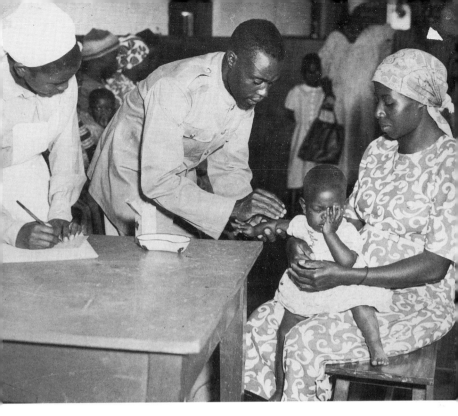

ABOVE. African clinic
BELOW. External view of African clinic

ABOVE. Street scene, Lusaka
BELOW. Victoria Falls

ABOVE. City Hall, Lusaka
BELOW. City Hall, Salisbury (Harare)

ABOVE. The African Hospital, Salisbury (Harare)
BELOW. The author and family

general manager of General Motors, who was on his way from America to South Africa, on the flying boat, to view the falls. When walking through the rain forest, which was alleged to be free of snakes because of the dampness, a six-foot cobra stood up on its tail and lunged at us, but did not, however, succeed in delivering a bite. This was the only occasion that a reptile had, in my experience, been aggressive, but a short while later the Northern Rhodesian government medical officer found a cobra attempting to get into his house through the gauze netting surrounding his veranda. He was attempting to shoot it with his handgun when the reptile spat into his face through the gauze and the venom entered his eyes. He came rushing to see me because of severe irritation in his eyes and he had acute conjunctivitis. In the age-old tradition, I washed out his eyes with fresh milk and to this day have not been able to understand why milk was traditionally advised in these cases rather than water or saline. He made a rapid recovery. Pythons were occasionally seen in the area, especially at the bottom of the falls. An encounter with a night adder at Kapiri Mposhi near Broken Hill, and the adventure with a python while in the army near Salisbury, have already been described. On the evening of the last day we were to spend in Central Africa, in Lusaka, a large gaboon viper was seen coiled up next to our sitting room door. It was dispatched forthwith with a convenient broom.

The time I spent in Livingstone and at Victoria Falls was undoubtedly the most interesting and enjoyable period of my service in Central Africa. It was a period in which I was involved in unusual and exciting events in quick succession. Important people from all over the world visited the falls and I was called upon to treat some very impressive individuals, including Mrs Macmillan, the wife of the British prime minister, who was staying at the hotel during a visit to Central Africa. One 'hallowed' guest at the hotel was the premier of South Africa. He arrived there in a luxurious viceregal train, which had been built by South African Railways for the king and queen's visit to South Africa about three years previously. Shortly after his arrival the hotel manager phoned me to seek my help in a quandary which had arisen. The premier, or a member of his entourage, had complained that the South African flag was not displayed on the flagpole in front of the hotel where the Union Jack was flying. My advice to the manager was that under no circumstances was the Union Jack to be replaced. As another flagpole was not available in Victoria Falls, with the help of the district engineer, the flagpole of the Railway Club in Livingstone was taken to the hotel and erected alongside the pole already there. The South African flag was hoisted on the pole so that both flags were kept flying and the impasse solved. I was told he declined to be served by African waiters and preferred to be attended by European stewards from his special train during his stay at the hotel.

A large proportion of the tourists at the hotel were Americans, who were very noisy. When they came in large numbers from a cruise ship calling at South African ports, not only would they fill all the hotel rooms, but their train in the adjacent station would be used to accommodate the overflow. They were unusually conscious of their health and I had many unnecessary calls. One gentleman, who was quartered on the train, sent for me because he thought he may have been bitten by a mosquito and wished to know what he should do to prevent himself developing 'some queer tropical disease'. When I explained that the charge for a visit from Livingstone was two guineas he brought out a wad of Rhodesian treasury notes and requested me to help myself. I managed to find two pound notes and then explained that I still required a two-shilling coin. His reply was that he did not worry about coins; he gave me a ten-pound note from his wad and declined to take any change!

Many years ago I remember reading a story by O'Henry entitled 'First Aid for Millionaires', but did not imagine that I would ever be involved in a practical instance of his theme. On a Saturday afternoon I was called to the outpatient department of the Livingstone Hospital to see an urgent case. It turned out to be an hysterical American woman demanding to return immediately to the United States to be back at home with her family. Her husband was very annoyed and pleaded with her, in vain, to be reasonable. It transpired that they were on a world tour and had been away from home for only about ten days when she became homesick. Her husband produced a wallet containing numerous attached worldwide air tickets, which he threw across the room, requesting to know what he was to do with them all, for they had cost him many thousands of dollars. I assured him that, on the production of a medical certificate from me stating that they were unable to complete the tour because of illness through no fault of their own, the fares would be refunded. They eventually left the hospital in a much happier state with the intention of arranging their immediate flight back to the United States.

On another occasion I had seen a television programme about an alcoholic entitled 'A Lost Weekend'. My American patient at Victoria Falls had lost a lot longer than that! I was called to see an American at the hotel who did not eat and refused to leave his bed. It transpired that he was a young man on an extended world tour accompanied by a paid companion. He was an alcoholic and his wealthy family had decided to send him on this tour in the vain hope that it would cure his addiction. On examination, my patient was completely unaware where he was or when he had left his home. He had a tremor and slurred speech. A bump under his mattress turned out to be a half-full bottle of gin. The companion informed me that they had left his home about eight days previously and that his charge was quite unaware of the period which had elapsed — a lost week. He was admitted to Livingstone Hospital as a case of delirium tremens, where he made a rapid, most likely temporary, recovery.

Numerous conferences were held at the hotel. One was held on the feasibility of creating a Central African Federation. It was attended by Roy Welensky as leader of the Northern Rhodesia Legislative Assembly, Godfrey Huggins, the prime minister of Southern Rhodesia, and Malcolm Barrow, leader of the Nyasaland Unofficials. It was interesting to note that there was not a single African among the delegations from the three territories. As far as I can recollect the conference achieved little more than a suggestion that further appeals be made to the United Kingdom government to negotiate the establishment of a Central African Federation with its own government.

The Local Authorities' Association of Southern Rhodesia held frequent, I think annual, conferences at the hotel — naturally in the interest of its parishioners! During one of these conferences I was called to the hotel to see a patient. On the way between the bridge and my destination I was hailed by a couple of men who requested a lift to the hotel. They explained they were delegates to the conference and that one of them was feeling faint from the heat, which was why they were asking for a lift. The one, who appeared to be foreign, said he was the mayor of a Rhodesian town and was of Greek extraction. He enquired if I was a delegate to the conference. When I explained that I was a Livingstone resident, he had the audacity to say that 'they' would save us from British domination and hoped the Central African Federation would soon be established. I was so flabbergasted that I refrained from telling him what I had on my mind.

Another unusual episode took place during a conference of Rotary International. The president and committee of the 'whole shooting match' were present and the president, who was an American, fell ill. A Rotary Club had been established in Livingstone about a year previously and I was asked to join as the 'leading' medical practitioner in the town. I declined the invitation on the grounds that I was not the leading practitioner; the only other two medical men, both Northern Rhodesia government doctors, declined to join on the same grounds. The chairman of the local branch approached me to attend the sick president at the hotel and, with obvious embarrassment, asked me not to mention that I was not a Rotarian. I acceded to his request. After I had examined and prescribed treatment for the VIP he invited me to have a drink with all the other important Rotarians standing around. One of the locals hurriedly advised me not to order an alcoholic drink because the great man was a teetotaller and disapproved of the use of alcohol. He mentioned (once again to the embarrassment of disconcerted local members) how lucky we were to be so well looked after by fellow Rotarians all over the world! No non-European was observed in this large gathering of Rotarians.

It was customary for recently-married European couples in both Rhodesias, and even further afield, to spend their honeymoon at the falls. I therefore became conversant with the medical problems confronting newlyweds. It was surprising how ignorant of sex some couples were. It was usually the male partner who took the sensuous pleasure out of their first night of marriage because of disregard of gentility. It gave me satisfaction to be able to advise these young couples how they should behave and prevent an unhappy union. In other cases it was a vaginal haemorrhage that required urgent attention. I always knew when I was attending to a honeymoon couple because of the vase of flowers placed in their rooms, a gesture which was not available to other guests.

African nationalism was developing in the three territories, though it is doubtful if it influenced the agitation by employees at the Victoria Falls Hotel to demand the right to wear *tackies* (a name given to canvas shoes with rubber soles). I personally agreed with their reasonable request, which was eventually granted. Apart from the waiters, none of the African workers at the hotel had shoes included in their uniforms; they were expected to pad silently along the corridors and in the rooms barefooted.

When the nationalist African National Congress was formed in Southern Rhodesia, its leaders were arrested. The active leaders of the party at Victoria Falls included hotel employees. The hotel manager was nonplussed when he learned that a couple of the quiet and unassuming members of his staff, including his own personal servant, had been arrested, while the loudmouthed threatening extroverts were left in peace. This did not surprise me following a similar experience we had at Broken Hill when our garden sweeper was found to be a union leader. It was at this time that the medical orderly employed in the railway surgery in Livingstone informed me that he had been offered the post of secretary (or some other high rank) of the African Railways Workers' Union. Because of the nature of his employment, I suggested it was inadvisable for him to become involved in active politics. Within a couple of days I received a threatening telegram from the African Railways Workers' Union warning me not to interfere in its union activities.

For many years an established means of transport at the Victoria Falls was the use of narrow-gauge small passenger trolleys on rails propelled by Africans. These trolleys were provided by the hotel to transport visitors from the hotel to the river and the falls. It was comparatively easy for the pushers to propel the trolleys on rails down to the river. All they had to do was hang on to the back of the trolley and apply the brakes when on the downward slope. The return trip from the river to the hotel was a totally different matter. The pushers had a hard job pushing the trolleys on the upward slope. The exertion required made them perspire freely and their heavy breathing was audible to the passengers. This form of transport had been in use for many years without any denunciatory opinion being made, but in the latter part of the fifth decade the manager of the hotel and the general manager of the railways began to receive letters from guests complaining about the employment of human beings to propel the trolleys. The truth of the matter was that being 'trolley boys' was the most popular occupation of all hotel employees. The job was not nearly as physically taxing as they made out. The heavy panting was made audible in order to secure a good gratuity at the journey's end. As a result of the criticism the use of this picturesque means of transport was discontinued and a small motorbus was provided instead. The hotel manager wisely preserved one of the trolleys; it was placed in the hotel garden where it can be seen to the present day.

A case was brought to my attention by the police of an African who had been taken on by the railways as a 'paint boy'. His first assignment was to paint the underside of the falls bridge. However, he found being perched about 300 feet above the river below too stressful. The foreman decided to charge him under the Master & Servants' Act for disobeying a legitimate order. I mention this episode not because of the ridiculous charge but because it was an illustration of racial intolerance.

I encountered numerous medical problems during my stay in Livingstone, but one in particular does not fade from my memory. I was called to the African hospital in Livingstone one day to see two patients from the Victoria Falls area. They were very jaundiced and semi-conscious. Within a matter of minutes, before I could examine them, they had died. During the next few hours another three patients were admitted from the same camp at Jafuta, a railway siding near the falls.

The camp was run by the Witwatersrand Native Labour Association, which recruited Africans in Central Africa for employment in the Witwatersrand gold mines. The present inmates, who were being properly fed and clothed in the camp

before being sent on to Johannesburg by rail, had been brought
overland from Angola. The camp was supervised by a local farmer
who was employed by the WNLA. The three more recently
admitted patients were also very ill and jaundiced. They had been
recruited in what was designated a yellow-fever area and I felt sure
I was dealing with an outbreak of yellow fever. They had stiff
necks and a lumbar puncture revealed a purulent cerebo-spinal
fluid which showed meningitis or inflammation of the meninges —
a membrane surrounding the brain. Microscopic examination of
the fluid revealed meningococci, so the diagnosis was meningococcal meningitis or spotted fever. The prevalent antibiotic was
M&B693, which was instilled into their cerebo-spinal fluid. Despite
treatment, two of them died; the other recovered.

I visited the camp the next day and had the alarming experience
of seeing an individual collapse while walking across the quad-
rangle separating the dormitories. He was dead when I got to him,
also in a matter of seconds. All camp inmates were immediately
given prophylactic M&B693 tablets. There were three further
cases, all of whom recovered after treatment and, following the
issue of M&B tablets, there were no further cases. I had not read
about such a severe outbreak of meningococcal meningitis before,
but an article in a medical journal published by a drugs company a
short time later stated that meningococcal meningitis was the most
frequent cause of sudden death in the United States army.

A yellow-fever area, so designated, was one in which the mouse
protection test was found to be positive in certain individuals or
monkeys living in the area. It was assumed that if individuals or
monkeys had been infected with the yellow-fever virus they would
have corresponding antibodies in their blood. The mouse protection test consisted of infecting the brains of laboratory mice with
the yellow-fever virus. They invariably died. However, if the blood
of the mice (and of individuals or monkeys) infected with the virus
contained antibodies to the disease, they recovered. Those areas in
which the mice recovered were designated as yellow-fever areas.
While yellow fever was prevalent in parts of South America and
caused problems in the building of the Panama Canal, as far as I
know, no case has ever been reported in Central Africa. The strict
controls we administered in the case of travellers, who were

required to have a valid certificate of yellow-fever inoculation, have therefore been discontinued.

The agitation for the establishment of a Central African state consisting of the two Rhodesias and Nyasaland was hotting up. Huggins and Welensky became very active in the pursuit of their ambition to create the state. They made frequent trips to the UK to negotiate with the British government. British colonial and dominion secretaries visited the territories to assess the proposal. I met Welensky in Livingstone on two occasions following his visits to the United Kingdom. On one occasion he had been given the full Astor treatment, including a royal breakfast at Buckingham Palace and a trip to Paris. He appeared to be walking on air following the indoctrination. Huggins and Roy were in favour of amalgamating the two Rhodesias on purely economic grounds, combining the industrial and agricultural wealth of Southern Rhodesia (with its European 'know how') with the mineral wealth, especially copper, of Northern Rhodesia. It was on the insistence of the UK government that Nyasaland was to be included in any deal.

My wife and I were fervently opposed to the idea of a federation. It was inconceivable to us that the Africans in Northern Rhodesia and Nyasaland could possibly accept the idea of joining Southern Rhodesia in any political grouping, whether it be amalgamation, federation or any other union. African nationalism had been developing in the territories. The African nationalist political parties in Southern Rhodesia were agitating for a constitution in which 'one man had one vote'. The nationalists in the other two territories were seeking independence under black governments. At that time these political demands were unthinkable to Europeans. The Africans in Livingstone were almost entirely against federation and minor demonstrations were held. One of their specious arguments against it was that God had created the three separate countries and it was sacrilege for anyone to suggest they should be amalgamated. The attitude of colonial government officials in Northern Rhodesia was ambivalent. They apparently had been instructed to encourage the establishment of the federation, but expressed personal misgivings when discussing the position in private.

Livingstone and the Central African Federation

The government of Southern Rhodesia under the premiership of Huggins strongly encouraged the formation of the federation and the idea was accepted by the majority of European residents in the territory. A referendum was to be held, and voters, who were almost entirely European, were asked to record their vote in favour of or against the proposed federation. For the first time in our lives my wife and I took part in politics and, on every appropriate occasion, advised our personal friends and residents on the southern bank of the Zambezi River to vote NO, despite their government's propaganda for them to vote YES. Our rhetoric and polemic arguments against the change were in vain. They voted by a two to one majority in favour. It was difficult to understand why Southern Rhodesian Europeans were in favour of joining the two neighbouring colonial territories in a federation. The reasons were complicated. Southern Rhodesia was a very British colony and, in the tradition of Rhodes, they visualized an enlarged territory under European control. There were obvious economic advantages, but their choice seemed irrational to us when the population of the proposed new federation would be increased by between four and five million Africans and about 50,000 Europeans. We were not impressed by the propaganda of its supporters, which consisted of repeated expressions of partnership between the races and the creation of a bulwark against the spread of communism in Central Africa.

Following the frequent going and coming of interested parties between the United Kingdom and Central Africa and the conclusion of protracted negotiations, the British government agreed to the establishment of the federation of Southern and Northern Rhodesia and Nyasaland, which came into being in 1953 with Britain retaining control of external affairs and legislation affecting Africans. The two northern territories remained under the protection of the Crown with governors and European-dominated legislative assemblies. At the outset we thought that it was unreasonable to expect these five governments to continue to work in union, without disruption and distrust, in the future. Mr Huggins, later Lord Malvern, became prime minister of the federal government with Roy Welensky as his minister of transport. Mr Garfield Todd, a liberal ex-missionary, replaced Mr Huggins as prime minister of Southern Rhodesia. All this political shillyshally did not affect us personally in any way and life in Livingstone continued to be pleasant and interesting. We had many good friends, mostly among government officials. Through our contact with the management of the Victoria Falls Hotel and the district commissioner in Livingstone, we had opportunities to meet important and interesting visitors to the vicinity. My wife and I were invited to have afternoon tea with Mr and Mrs Attlee in Livingstone when he was prime minister of the UK. They were a charming couple and it soon became obvious that Mr Attlee was not photogenic, for he had an outstandingly impressive personality which did not manifest itself when he appeared on television. I had the privilege of sitting next to Lord Douglas-Home at a government luncheon party when he was dominion secretary. He was an erudite, charming English gentleman, but like most politicians or statesmen, had an over optimistic opinion of the economic future of the proposed federation of Central Africa. Little did I realize that he would soon be the British prime minister.

I also had the opportunity to meet an Israeli ambassador who had previously been a bank manager in London. He told me he had interviewed Dr Verwoerd, the South African prime minister, in Pretoria the previous week, when Dr Verwoerd had informed him that the Europeans would be able to maintain their dominant role in South Africa under the apartheid system for at least another ten years, but was unable to prognosticate what would happen after that time! Dr Verwoerd was assassinated during a debate in the South African parliament a short while later, so would never know that the minority European government had remained in power in that country for another 28 years.

I had frequent contact with Africans on both sides of the Zambezi and was able to ascertain a cross section of their opinions. The Southern Rhodesian Africans did not seem to take much interest in the federation and looked upon it as a European matter. The Africans in Northern Rhodesia, however, had been pro-nationalist and anti-federalist from the outset and were becoming more so. They were not slow to express their opinions. As we anticipated being in Livingstone for some years to come, we decided to build our own house in the town. When the building was nearing completion, two African labourers employed by the builder approached me and suggested that we were 'misguided to build the house because an African government will be taking over the territory in the near future and all European property will be given to the indigenous population'. Though we were aware that African nationalist politicians in both Rhodesias were giving their uninformed followers assurances they must surely have known they would be unable to achieve, it nevertheless gave us a sense of insecurity, which resulted in our selling the house.

On stopping at a ganger's cottage on one of my trips up the line, I heard African employees expressing dissatisfaction with their lot and complaining that they did all the work on the railways but did not own them. In this respect, despite all the talk of partnership and the British government's claims to be guarding the interests of the African population, the Rhodesia Railways did not employ any black firemen, guards or shunters. It was only a semi-skilled job to be a fireman and fling coal into a locomotive's firebox when the temperature in the shade outside was over 90 degrees. Because of the recent war and the continuing world demand for copper, the railways were always short of personnel. All British railwaymen willing to emigrate to Rhodesia, at a vastly increased rate of pay, had already been recruited, and this applied equally to Ireland. When I was in Livingstone, plane loads of Dutchmen, who had worked in the Dutch East Indies before they fought for and lost the country, arrived at the airport. They were railway recruits and each individual had to be medically examined by me to ascertain his fitness for employment. They were well educated, impressive young men and most of them gave up their employment on the railways as soon as their contracts expired. Unfortunately, the opportunity was not taken at this time, when there was full European employment, to offer these jobs to suitable Africans who were available. I once asked an African employee how they would manage to run the railways if and when they took over, given that a fireman had to serve a seven-year apprenticeship on the footplate before he became an engine driver. The unexpected reply was that it may take a European seven years to become a driver, but an African could accomplish the apprenticeship in seven weeks! At times Africans could be very annoying because of their lack of understanding and unreasonable demands, but no doubt was left in my mind about their dislike of federation and their desire to be self-governing.

In the meantime events had moved on in the local region. The aerodrome at Livingstone had been completed and had become a busy international airport. It was given a gala opening to which aircraft and persons involved in aviation worldwide were invited. The airport at Victoria Falls was closed and BOAC used Constellations, Hermes and later Comet aircraft for the South African run, which called at Livingstone both south and northbound. At the opening of the aerodrome Lord Longford, the British minister responsible for aviation, asked one of the local staff how many residents lived in Livingstone. As I happened to be standing nearby, he told him that I was the local doctor and would know more about it! I readily informed Lord Longford that the local population was about 5000. He gruffly pointed to the large number of African spectators observing events from beyond a high wire fence nearby. I lamely had to state that the number of Africans resident in the area was not known to me, or for that matter to anyone else, because accurate population statistics were difficult to obtain in a relatively mobile community. He noted my discomfort, snorted and walked off. Unfortunately, the whole conversation was overheard by a newspaper reporter and reported verbatim in the local press the next day.

With the advent of federation, my appointment as Southern Rhodesia's government medical officer came to an end, but the Colonial Development Corporation appeared on the scene. This was a brainchild of the UK government to develop agriculture in various British colonial territories in Africa in order to improve the standard of living. The failures of its groundnut scheme in Tanganyika and of its poultry-development scheme in the Gambia were well known. It now intended to grow maize on a large scale in the fertile lands of northern Bechuanaland. The conception was admirable and I was approached by the local director of the scheme to advise on any medical problems that might arise. It was not long before one of its representatives brought me the plans for a cottage hospital it intended to build in the region it was developing. As he was not even sure of the eventual number of individuals who would be living in the area, without further enquiry I immediately condemned the scheme as unrealistic. I was informed that expensive agricultural machinery had been brought to the inaccessible site at the cost of millions of pounds. I did not at any time visit the intended development, but a number of bureaucrats who were in charge of cooperatives in the UK made numerous visits to its local headquarters in Livingstone. However, for reasons unknown to me, the scheme never really got off the ground and was abandoned. All the valuable agricultural machinery was bought by the local foundry at knockdown prices. To my mind, this was an example of how easy it is to spend other people's money, in this case the United Kingdom taxpayers'. It was also an illustration of how a beneficial development project started at the top and went down when it should have commenced at the bottom and built up!

The medical faculty of the Afrikaans University of Pretoria in South Africa made a request to come up to Northern Rhodesia to study tropical diseases; a party of about 20 students, under their professor of medicine, duly arrived at Victoria Falls and set up a camp. We were invited to a *braaivleis* (barbecue) as only the Afrikaans can produce. It was a most enjoyable feast of their special sausages, meat and cooked mealie-meal (finely-ground maize). The next day I took them around the hospital to point out the suitable cases for study. While seeing patients in the African hospital, the professor made the incredible observation that the diseases of these people were different from those of Europeans. I was aware from my experience of Afrikaners in Broken Hill that they did not regard Africans as human compared with whites, but to hear this opinion expressed by a professor, an academician, left me flabbergasted. The police training camp in Livingstone was able to put on a retreat ceremony as good as that of any of the best regiments in the UK. I therefore asked my good friend Norman Brodie, who was in charge of the police, to arrange for an emergency ceremony the next day. The whole party of visiting Afrikaners accepted the invitation to attend. One of its highlights for me was to observe their attitude and the look on their faces as they saw Africans handling firearms and drilling with precision to the accompaniment of their own impeccable brass band. It was amusing to hear their remarks, such as 'Ag man! What do you think of these Kaffirs? It must have taken a long time for them to learn this.'

Livingstone Hospital was a very busy, efficient establishment with completely separate European and African sections. It was managed by a medical superintendent and two matrons, one in charge of each of the two sections. How different it was from the cumbersome administration of hospitals in the UK today, with their plethora of accountants and other unqualified staff! As was the practice of the time, the hospitals were divided into male and female wards and, as in all the smaller colonial hospitals, a qualified dispenser/secretary attended to the dispensing and accounting requirements. SRNs (State Registered Nurses) and the matron, with auxiliaries, made up the nursing staff in the European section of about 40 beds, and a matron with one SRN, aided by trained African medical orderlies, attended to the patients in the 300 beds in the African section, which was always overcrowded. Many of the patients there were accommodated on blankets on the floor between the beds. There were no consultants and the government medical officers and I made up the complete medical staff in the area. A young houseman, or recently-qualified student, from a South African medical school was also stationed in the African hospital. We managed to cope with all cases requiring medical or surgical attention and rarely had to send a difficult case to Bulawayo in Southern Rhodesia or Lusaka in Northern Rhodesia, where large provincial hospitals with full consultant staffs were available.

It was customary for senior staff to serve the Christmas Day meal to the hospital servants. While I was carving the turkey on Christmas Day 1948, three unconscious European patients were admitted to the hospital — two with cerebral malaria and one with a severe typhoid infection. Typhoid was perhaps the most distressing condition we were called upon to treat. The patient would be highly toxic, with a rising temperature, severe diarrhoea and bleeding from the intestine. Despite intensive nursing care, most cases were fatal. I derived great satisfaction a few years later from being able to treat these cases with the new antibiotic, chloramphenicol. The first person to be treated with chloramphenicol in the hospital was a young European girl admitted into my care with a severe attack of typhoid. Within 48 hours she was sitting up and smiling — a miraculous cure! It was not unusual for me and members of the nursing staff to be up most of the night attending to an acute surgical case or blocked labour, have a bath and attend to our routine chores at 8.00 a.m. the next morning. Apart from leaves, I was personally on call for 24 hours a day every day of the year. Although we were members of an exclusive boat club, I did not have the pleasure of an outing up the river because it was essential for me to be at the end of a telephone. These were the days before sophisticated means of communication. It amuses me to read of complaints by modern young doctors because they are on call for over 72 hours a week!

Because the Colonial Office was finding it difficult to recruit nursing staff, an arrangement was made for the African hospital to be staffed by nuns of the Franciscan Order. It was my first experience of working with nuns, and I was slightly apprehensive, but they turned out to be very efficient, dedicated, nursing sisters with a keen sense of humour. It surprised me to discover how interested they were in their materialistic requirements. They apparently did not receive any tangible cash reward, but at the outset they were not satisfied with the thin mattresses supplied to the previous two nursing sisters, and also complained about the refrigerator provided because it was too small to hold bottles of beer and other liquid refreshments. A larger one was installed. They also had a motorcar at their disposal. The young houseman living in an adjoining cottage complained about the noise made at night by the singing and noisy revelry coming from the nuns' abode. The only complaint I had against them was that at certain times of the day, when the Angelus or other bells rang, they dropped whatever they were doing and went off to pray. Their main concern seemed to be to convert dying African patients to Christianity. I could never make up my mind whether this was done from purely religious conviction, or if they thought their passage to their God in heaven would be made easier when their time came if they had converted a large number of souls on earth. Anyway, it supported my personal view that most religious belief is based on fear of the unknown following death.

My limited experience of missionaries' achievements in Central Africa up to that time reminded me of the curate's egg — good in parts. My interest was naturally in the medical missionaries who did good work treating Africans in remote areas. In some instances, a condition such as yaws — a venereal disease resulting in sores scattered over the body — was treated by giving various types of injection, which cured the condition like magic, but then it was suggested to trusting, naïve Africans that a supernatural religious being had cured their complaint. There were missionary (and secularist) doctors who dedicated their lives to caring for their unfortunate fellow men in remote isolated areas where diseases such as sleeping sickness or leprosy were prevalent and at times they contracted these diseases themselves. Unfortunately I do not remember their names, but they certainly performed a much more useful purpose than a well-publicized leprologist in North Africa whose most outstanding accomplishment, according to a colleague of mine who visited his hospital, was his management of the media.

With the help of her daughter and son-in-law, an American woman ran a missionary orphanage for African children in the vicinity of Livingstone. I had delivered her daughter's babies and whenever the family came to me for medical attention they always brought me a small paper packet of home-grown tomatoes, a gesture I much appreciated. The mother often told me that they were short of money for running the mission, but in the past God had always provided, as he would in the future! On their way to the United States on leave one year they broke their journey in Johannesburg, from where they phoned me with an urgent request for a medical certificate to prove they were fit and not suffering from any infectious disease. They asked me to send it posthaste to the Carlton Hotel, Johannesburg. The amusing aspect of this story is that the Carlton was a five-star hotel in which I would never have dared to have stayed because of the expense!

While stationed in Livingstone, my wife received a request from the government to inaugurate a society for the non-racial care of the blind in Northern Rhodesia. She had a busy time establishing the organization and received due recognition for her success. The district commissioner then came up with a somewhat odd proposal. Since up until now there had been so little social contact between the races and Africans had only been entertained in the homes of government officials, as an unprecedented local gesture, would we, he asked, as private individuals, consider entertaining an educated African politician in our home? We readily acceded to his request and in due course invited the recommended local politician to a dinner party. The other four guests were government officials and their wives. It is interesting to note that, from our point of view, the party was a success, but the next day our usually placid African cook was very upset and rebuked us for having an African as a guest in our house. He was furious and stated that he was employed to work for an *Unshlungu* (European) and not a *Munhu* (African). The gentleman we entertained was eventually made a member of the Monckton Commission, which reported on the progress of the federation. When we met him about ten years later in Lusaka, after Northern Rhodesia had been granted independence under African rule, he seemed reluctant to recall the occasion on which we had entertained him in Livingstone.

As a developing country, it was relatively easy for enterprising individuals to achieve commercial success and profit in Northern Rhodesia. I knew a moulder who was employed on the mine at Broken Hill. After the Second World War ended, he and his brother settled in Livingstone where they started up an iron foundry; they requested my advice on any medical problems they were likely to encounter. The mines on the Copperbelt used iron mill balls of varying diameters to crush the copper ore. These iron balls were imported from Belgium and these enterprising young men, who experimented with moulding them in their factory, discovered they could produce a similar article at about one-third of the price being paid for the imported product. They clinched a contract for the supply of mill balls to the copper mines and within a few weeks their factory was working three shifts each day and sending truckloads of the product they produced to the Copper-belt. They went around buying up scrap iron in both Rhodesias, which was smelted to be moulded into mill balls. Within three years they had made a fortune and emigrated to the United States. I am relating this story because their success was undoubtedly due to the Africans' strong desire to work with *simbe* (iron). They worked extremely hard and with obvious satisfaction. Traditionally, metalworkers producing spears or cooking pots are highly respected members of a tribe. The iron foundry manufactured three-legged African cooking pots in addition to the mill balls.

The Zambezi Saw Mills, which operated a private railway with a 100-mile track running into the adjacent hardwood forests was, along with the railway workshops, one of the largest commercial enterprises in Livingstone. It employed hundreds of African labourers and ran a hospital, with a full-time doctor, deep in the forest. It produced hardwood railway sleepers and turned the offcuts into parquet flooring. I was its medical adviser in Livingstone. When travelling into the forest, its European members of staff were accommodated in a special coach, while the African workers sat on the logs in the open trucks.

It was 1959. I had reached the age and served the requisite number of years to qualify for retirement. Many years of employment in a profession that necessitated being on call for 24 hours a day and working very hard had inclined me towards a change to a less demanding type of medical practice. A recent advertisement in a medical journal for the post of regional government medical officer in Umtali, a pleasant town in the eastern district of Southern Rhodesia, appealed to me and I decided to visit it to ascertain the details of the job. On the way to Umtali it was necessary to spend the day in Salisbury. By coincidence I met two old friends while walking in the main street. This chance meeting was to change my future professional career. The first friend I met was my old bank manger from Livingstone. He had been transferred to Umtali, but had recently been transferred again from Umtali to Salisbury. On hearing of my intention to move to Umtali, he unhesitatingly advised me against it because of the climate. He described how it was an attractive place for a tourist to visit, but situated as it was in a valley surrounded by hills, the heat in the town became very oppressive in the summer months. If one lived higher up the hills it was cooler, but there was usually a morning mist which persisted until midday. The next person I happened to chance upon was my old friend John Board, who had been the government medical officer in Broken Hill when we were stationed there. He had since retired and was currently employed as deputy medical officer of health in Salisbury. When I explained why I was on my way to Umtali, he said that I was the very chap they were looking for to be their senior clinical medical officer in the city's Department of Health, to take charge of their hospitals and clinics. He took me to his office and introduced me to the medical officer of health. I accepted the offer and was eventually appointed as the incumbent of the post. My wife was pleased when she heard of our intended move to Salisbury.

As in Broken Hill, we had experienced a happy and interesting stay in Livingstone — perhaps more so than in Broken Hill — and would miss our friends, particularly Vincent Tones, the manager of the Victoria Falls Hotel, and his wife. We spent our last night in the hotel's royal suite and next day set out for Salisbury in our two cars, with our young son, a servant who had asked to continue working for us in Salisbury, and our two dogs. We broke our journey at Kafue, where we spent the night at a modest roadhouse hotel, and eventually reached Salisbury the next day.

When we crossed the Zambezi River at Chirundu we experienced our first and (for us personally) only tangible benefit of federation. There were no longer any immigration or customs' formalities to be laboriously negotiated between the two territories.

5

Salisbury and the End of Federation

O n our arrival in Salisbury our first impression of change was the altered skyline. Attractive new tall buildings in the city centre transfigured the topographical nature of the locality, but this was not the only change. The federation had been in existence for six years and its economic success had brought enormous benefits to Southern Rhodesia, particularly to Salisbury. The federal authorities had mistakenly decided to make Salisbury the federal capital. It had been a psychological and tangible blunder not to have distributed the advantages more evenly in all three territories; rather than follow the examples of Ottawa in Canada or Canberra in Australia they had concentrated most of the benefits in one territory. When we were living in Livingstone, before the establishment of the federation, we had thought that the new capital would be in Kalomo, a small town on the escarpment near Livingstone and the border of the Rhodesias. It has a higher altitude than Livingstone and the climatic conditions, with a lower temperature, would have made it a most desirable site for the capital city, but it was not to be!

No longer was Salisbury the gracious, sedate capital city of Southern Rhodesia it had been before the war, when the majority of its inhabitants consisted of civil servants and their families. Nor was it the fascinating, exuberant, garrison town in which we had been stationed before I became the railways' medical officer in Broken Hill. It was now an attractive, prosperous city with lush

suburbs. With an adequate rainfall, most gardens were conspicu-
ously productive and attractive. It was alleged to have the most
equable climate in the world, the temperature rarely going below
50° or above 90°F. As one American visitor remarked, 'You have
the climate California advertises!' It was now the capital city of
two governments, the Southern Rhodesian government under the
premiership of Edgar Whitehead, and the federal government with
Roy Welensky as its prime minister. Both parliaments and
administrations were accommodated in the city, as were the
numerous foreign embassies established there since the advent of
the federation. A large manufacturing base had also been established locally to meet the increased demand for manufactured
goods, which was another benefit bestowed by the federation. The
Northern Rhodesian copper mining companies had transferred
their administrative departments to the city; in fact one of the
largest and most attractive buildings was built and occupied by
one of their companies.

We soon settled down in Salisbury, re-establishing contact with
old friends and making many new ones. Because of the large
turnover of Europeans at this time through immigration and
emigration, it was not difficult to choose and purchase the house
we wanted. It was a typical double-storeyed English country
residence, quite unlike the popular split-level ranch-style house so
popular and sought after in the city. We built a very adequate
swimming pool and changing room in our garden and spent most
weekends entertaining our friends with swimming and gin-and-
tonic parties. Social life became very hectic, with frequent visits to
cinemas or theatres where leading overseas' actors could be seen
and heard. Numerous house parties, especially tennis parties, were
held in the gardens of our friends who possessed tennis courts.
With a glorious climate and willing black servants, these were
indeed halcyon days for Europeans resident in Central Africa,
particularly in Salisbury. However, our initial enthusiasm was
dampened slightly by the person fitting the curtains in our new
house remarking that, 'You obviously have faith in the future of
this territory. We arrived here from England five years' ago and
have decided to move on again because we are pessimistic about
the future.' Our house had been built by an English civil engineer

about four years previously. He had been employed by a large engineering concern and had decided to sell up and transfer his interests to New Zealand.

We had not been there long when we noticed a marked change in the composition of the city's residents. The stolid, paternalistic, likeable old colonial Rhodesians had become so diluted by new immigrants that their presence was barely discernible. African citizens had undergone a complete transformation. No longer did they appear to be so servile; and numerous suited, well-shod African gentlemen were to be seen thronging the city centre and mingling with the crowds. Indeed many were better dressed than the Europeans. African females were conspicuous by their absence. During working hours, large numbers of Africans could be seen sitting on a low wall surrounding the central post office building avidly reading the daily newspaper, which was ostensibly produced for the interest of Europeans.

In the postwar years the Southern Rhodesian government encouraged the immigration of white kinsfolk into the territory, allegedly for their skills but in reality to increase the European population. In the early 1950s the surge of immigrants was so large that their numbers had to be controlled. There was an influx of white South Africans into Rhodesia following the success of the Afrikaner National Party in the South African elections, and it was feared that they would upset the balance between United Kingdom and South African residents. The government's promotion of immigration from the United Kingdom was such a success that Salisbury City Council had to provide special prefabricated buildings in the city in which to accommodate them temporarily. At the time British politicians openly stated that one of the main purposes of establishing the Central African Federation had been to build a strong Central African state to resist South African expansionism to the north. During the immigration boom a large number of South African medical practitioners settled in Salisbury. While I would not criticize their clinical ability, their medical etiquette left a lot to be desired. Some of them openly engaged in the practice of fee-sharing and few of them joined the salaried government or local authority medical services, which attended mainly to the needs of Africans who, with few exceptions, were too poor to pay for medical attention. They preferred to become general practitioners or consultants in the city centre where they benefited from the affluent, fee-paying European section of the community.

My wife became an honorary teacher at a college established and run by Jesuits for Africans in the Salisbury area. She taught typing, shorthand, simple bookkeeping and office routine. She also typed stencils of books that were otherwise unobtainable to the students. She thought that her students were keen to learn and advance themselves and that many of them were more efficient than European office workers, but when they graduated from the college few were able to obtain employment because of racial prejudice. Although no Papists ourselves, we were impressed by the Jesuits — Catholic intellectuals frowned on by the present pope — who gave unstinting, dedicated service to the education and advancement of Africans.

In my job as senior clinical medical officer for the Salisbury City Council I was in charge of the African and European hospitals for infectious diseases. The former had 500 beds and the latter 40 beds. I was also in charge of all the council's public-health clinics, as well as the health visitors. When I took over, all the health visitors and sisters in charge of clinics and hospital wards were European. Two other European clinical medical officers were employed in the department.

Having retired from Livingstone because of the onerous nature of my professional life there, I had anticipated a much easier time working in a mainly administrative post in Salisbury. It was ironic that our arrival in the city coincided with the outbreak of a severe polio epidemic. The wards in the European hospital rapidly began to fill with patients with varying degrees of paralysis. The patients with paralysis of the muscles of the respiratory system were nursed in artificial respirators commonly known as iron lungs. Fortunately, the matron and a nursing sister at the hospital had attended a special course in the United Kingdom on the management of respirators and the special nursing requirements of patients being treated in them. On entering the hospital the swooshing sound of the respirators could be heard in most parts of the building — a modern isolation hospital with airy single rooms and wide airy corridors. The majority of patients recovered partially or completely from their paralysis.

Poliomyelitis is an infectious disease, but most people infected with the virus merely have an influenza-like illness without paralysis. What struck me about this epidemic was that it was almost entirely confined to young adult Europeans. The number of polio cases in the African infectious diseases' hospital remained low. Over the months and years it was noted that practically all the African cases of poliomyelitis occurred in young children under the age of two years. Among Africans the disease was a true infantile paralysis, as it was known in years gone by. The difference in the ages at which Europeans and Africans contracted the disease most likely resulted from their different standards of hygiene. African infants crawling around on unclean floors or soil became infected by swallowing the polio virus from contaminated hands; they either developed infantile paralysis or acquired a lifelong immunity to the disease. European children brought up in clean hygienic conditions were less frequently infected and so did not develop a lifelong immunity. Hence the preponderance of adults among the unfortunate patients. Also, infected Europeans were most likely to suffer paralysis if they were physically exhausted. This was exemplified a short while later when refugees from the Congo developed the complaint in larger numbers than expected and were admitted to our hospital in Salisbury. Of course all this is now only of historical interest because the disease has been eradicated through immunization with the Salk and Sabin vaccines.

By far the majority of patients admitted to the African hospital were suffering from pulmonary tuberculosis. This was originally a European disease, but was now prevalent in the African population due to the lack of a 'herd' immunity. It was not unusual to have acute cases of galloping consumption, as it was known many years ago in Europe, admitted to the wards. Fortunately the disease had now become amenable to chemotherapy. All African males entering the city to seek work were obliged to have a mass miniature X-ray of the chest before the issue of a work permit.

Measles in a child suffering from kwashiorkor, a debilitating protein and vitamin deficiency caused by an inadequate diet, was the most worrying infectious disease admitted to the hospital. Despite all treatment, including antibiotics and vitamins, the condition had a high mortality rate; during measles epidemics we would have up to four deaths a day. It was extremely depressing trying to treat these cases, which did not respond to any available medication. Measles could also be very serious in African adults who had recently migrated to the city from remote areas. This was because, unlike Europeans, they had had no immunity to the disease passed on from their mothers. A section of the hospital was reserved for the treatment of venereal diseases. The patients here were no longer infected with indigenous venereal diseases such as yaws, but were usually in the advanced stages of European-type infections such as syphilis or gonorrhoea and could not therefore be treated as outpatients.

Despite employing African servants to cook and serve their food, and to look after their children, the average European resident was under the impression that infectious diseases had originated from the 'lazy', 'unclean', 'unreliable' Africans. Nothing could be further from the truth. It was the European settlers who introduced many of these diseases into Africa and it was the unfortunate indigenous population who suffered most because of their lack of immunity.

Though less exciting than my busy life in Livingstone had been, my professional work in the hospitals and clinics run by the Salisbury City Council turned out to be interesting and rewarding. In due course I was promoted to the post of deputy medical officer of health and, in addition to being in charge of hospitals and clinics, I also became responsible for supervising the environmental health department. I found it amusing to have the foods advertised on television each night analysed the following day; we were often able to prove that their advertised claims were fictitious. The miscreants would be charged in the courts and appropriately fined. One well-known beverage, advertised as an orange drink, was found to contain no orange juice whatsoever. Following the prosecution it was advertised as 'the drink which tastes like orange'. Local butchers were fined for having an insufficient percentage of meat in their sausages, and a well-known brand of coffee was found to be mostly chicory.

As acting medical officer of health I had to attend Health Committee and council meetings; I found this aspect of my work unpleasant. It was the first time I had come into contact with politicians and I was not impressed by their machinations. The councillors, who were mainly businessmen or accountants, gave me the impression, rightly or wrongly, that they were there to serve their own interests — they were so obviously populists. The mayor, who was Greek, was the owner of a grocery shop. Council meetings were invariably preceded by a meeting of councillors and chief officers in the mayor's parlour, where alcoholic drinks were freely available. It was at these gatherings that practically all our council contacts were made and most of our business was conducted. The Health Committee's published minutes bore no relation to what was actually said at the meetings and it was boring to have to sit through the stage-managed monthly council meetings, the deliberations of which would be reported under large headlines in the next morning's newspaper. There were no black councillors or senior council officials. The town clerk's department was manifestly subservient to the councillors; I avoided their dreary company as far as possible in the course of my duties.

Because Salisbury was much larger than Livingstone and our circumstances had changed, we did not come into contact with many local or visiting politicians, but I did see my old friend Roy Welensky at his official residence and at his private house. It was disappointing to realize that he was no longer the idealistic liberal I had known when he first began his political career in Broken Hill; but his dynamic, outstanding personality was still apparent. Most Europeans, and increasing numbers of Africans, were becoming politically conscious and depended on the media for keeping up with the momentous political changes taking place in Central Africa at the time. I did, however, find time to attend advertised meetings addressed by party political leaders.

A political meeting addressed by the prime minister of Southern Rhodesia, Edgar Whitehead, was interesting in two respects. First, his speech largely consisted of a knowledgeable analysis of the political situation in the country and appeared to suggest that he had a genuine desire to promote the advancement of the Africans. I would describe him as a liberal academic. The second interesting point about this meeting was the presence of white morons in the audience who persisted in barracking the speaker with such remarks as, 'What do you pay your garden Kaffir, hey Edgar?' On another occasion I attended a meeting addressed by Winston Field, the leader of the opposition Dominion Party, later to become the extreme right-wing Rhodesian Front. He seemed to be a pleasant enough individual, but I was unimpressed by his speech, which was almost entirely devoted to criticizing the United Nations, the British government, and the Southern Rhodesian government, which were all too liberal and pro-African for his liking.

In the meantime, African nationalism was growing rapidly, political violence was on the increase, and intimidation of the African population by extreme nationalists was becoming more widespread in the three federal territories.

A short while before we arrived in Salisbury, in 1959, the African National Congress, which advocated true partnership regardless of race, had been banned by Whitehead because it was considered to be subversive and 500 members were detained. Political violence in Nyasaland became so severe that federal troops and police from Southern Rhodesia were sent to the territory to maintain law and order. It was now 1960 and, with the steady advance of African influence in Northern Rhodesia and Nyasaland, Welensky stepped up his ranting and raving against the British government. At this time Mr Macmillan was the British prime minister and Mr Iain Macleod his colonial secretary. They were both left-wing Conservatives, which did not appeal to Welensky, who was accusing British politicians and officials of being evasive and dishonest in their negotiations with the federal government.

The granting of independence by the British government to various African countries (such as the Gold Coast, Nigeria, Kenya and Tanganyika) naturally made the African nationalists in the federation impatient to achieve their own independence. The British government, with the eventual consent of the federal government, decided to appoint a commission to report on the future of the federation. The commission, under the chairmanship of the well-known English politician and lawyer, Lord Monckton, who had been adviser to Edward VIII at the time of his abdication,

111

consisted of representatives of all five governments concerned. The commission visited all three federal territories and reported its findings within the year. Though one of its recommendations was that secession should be allowed, Welensky objected on the grounds that this was not in their terms of reference. Another of its recommendations was that the federation should continue, but with increased African participation in government to ensure its survival. Unless blacks and whites were given parity in the federal Parliament, early termination would be inevitable, for economic advancement was not a substitute for political progress. The majority of Europeans in Southern Rhodesia, however, seemed unconcerned about the federation or its future. Personally, we were grateful to read the Monckton Commission's findings, for it reassured us that this was the beginning of the end of federation.

Since Roy Welensky first mentioned the concept to me in Broken Hill more than 15 years previously, I had not changed my opinion about the Central African Federation; as far as we were concerned, it was a futile political venture. As I mentioned before, it was too much to expect the two northern territories, where the number of European settlers was negligible, to join up with Southern Rhodesia, which had a minority European government. It is unfortunate that the Northern and Southern Rhodesian politicians who originally contemplated the scheme (and convinced gullible British politicians of the economic benefits to be gained by the union of the two territories) did not anticipate the political repercussions that would ensue. In addition, it was unlikely that the five governments concerned, each with different attitudes and expectations, would ever be able to reconcile their heterogeneity.

The federal government's slogan was 'partnership of the races'. The only individual who defined the meaning of partnership was Huggins who, in his now infamous statement, compared it to the partnership of the 'horse and its rider'. Needless to say the African was the horse! The federal government Cabinet included black members and, for the first six years of federal rule, the African community made steady progress towards the breakdown of racial discrimination. My eldest son had won a bursary to attend the recently-established University College of Rhodesia and Nyasaland in Salisbury. It turned out to be an oasis where there was complete integration of the races, even to the extent of white and black students sharing the same hostels. Certain hotels in the city were allowed to admit members of all races. Segregation in shops, post offices and other public places where Africans were served at separate counters or windows gradually disappeared, and black scholars were being accepted in private schools.

Despite all the federal rhetoric about partnership and African advancement in the city, the following episode illustrated the idiocy of official social and economic segregation. We employed a builder, who had recently immigrated from Kent in England, to panel the internal walls of our house and redecorate the exterior of the property. While the work was being carried out with the help of two African assistants, a building inspector noted that one of the African assistants was painting an outside wall of the house. The builder was charged and fined for employing a black person to perform artisan's work in a white suburb!

Various political activities and changes over the previous years had played their part in creating this political situation in Southern Rhodesia. Sir Godfrey Huggins, later to become Lord Malvern, had been prime minister since 1933 — the longest serving premier in the British Empire. Although he was not a racist, he was, as I mentioned earlier, a safe politician without charisma. He had in fact been a surgeon in Salisbury for many years before entering politics. Like most of his thinking white countrymen, he visualized a time when the blacks would eventually take over the government of the territory, but certainly not in the foreseeable future. In 1953 he resigned and became prime minister of the new federal government.

Sir Godfrey was succeeded by Mr Garfield Todd, an impressive-looking man with a gift of the gab who had come to Rhodesia from New Zealand as a missionary. He genuinely and openly wished to promote the Africans' political, economic and social advancement but, as prime minister, had to be tough to maintain law and order and had to accommodate an overwhelmingly European electorate. As a result, the black community and the more moderate whites were disappointed when he failed to accomplish the changes he was expected to achieve. By 1958 the majority of the white electorate considered it undesirable to have a negrophile prime minister. His colleagues in the United Federal Party, which had been led by Roy Welensky in Northern Rhodesia and now had common purpose in both Rhodesias, decided to ease him out. The campaign within the party was led by Mr Fletcher, a Cabinet minister in the Todd government, who succeeded in getting him removed from the party leadership and ousted as prime minister. Todd, the liberal, and Welensky, who had developed right-wing tendencies, did not get on with each other; it was thought that behind the scenes Welensky had encouraged Todd's dismissal. By the time I met Roy Welensky in Salisbury, his interests were mainly directed towards promoting Anglo-American and other big mining-company concerns. Todd was more interested in the welfare of the African people.

Todd was succeeded by Sir Edgar Whitehead, now back in Southern Rhodesia after having retired from politics and from his post as federal ambassador in Washington. On his return he was defeated when he stood as a United Federal Party candidate in a Bulawayo by-election, but this was followed by a general election in which he was elected to parliament.

Significantly, the right-wing Dominion Party did unexpectedly well in the election and recorded as many votes, but not seats, as the United Federal Party. Sir Edgar, an obese, introspective, academic politician, also genuinely wished to help African advancement, but lacked charisma and was constrained by the European electorate.

In addition to banning the African National Congress, soon after becoming prime minister he also introduced repressive legislation, including the Preventive Detention Act, which authorized the detention of individuals without trial, and another act under which a 'native' could be prosecuted for undermining the authority of any government officer or official. In the course of time other black nationalist parties arose and were banned. Further restrictive legislation was passed and African leaders were detained. Sir Robert Tredgold, who was now chief justice of the federation, resigned in protest against these repressive acts because they interfered with the freedom of the individual. Nevertheless, as described before, it was under the Whitehead government that racial discrimination was gradually eradicated.

As ordinary citizens, we were bombarded with propaganda from politicians and the media about the need for Southern Rhodesia to be granted independence from Britain. As far as I was aware, the territory had been granted internal self-government in 1923, but they were worried about the reserve powers Britain retained to veto discriminatory legislation and control foreign affairs. When not blathering about the 'need to keep up civilized standards', individual Europeans also took up the call for independence. For our part, we were happy to retain the United Kingdom connection because, like most of the black population, we erroneously thought that the British people and parliament would, if need be, interfere to defend our rights as individuals. We thought that the main reason for the Rhodesian government's eagerness for independence was its fear that African leaders and people would look to Britain for support in their ambition to obtain a one man one vote elected government. I had little opportunity to discuss the political situation with Africans, for most of the educated Africans with whom I came into contact (members of my staff) were practically all Nyasas. I never discovered why so many of the educated black people working in Rhodesia came from Nyasaland, but presume it was because the various missionary centres active in that territory, such as Livingstonia run by the Church of Scotland, produced large numbers of trained Africans.

On driving home from work one evening, I found the roads leading into the city centre blocked by hundreds (perhaps thousands) of African women demonstrating outside the central police station. I cannot recollect what the protest was about, but was surprised to see African females now overtly taking part in the African nationalist movement, or 'struggle' as they described it.

The wearing of uniforms or emblems by African nationalists was banned by the government. When I noted that a large proportion of the African hospital staff had started wearing fur hats on arrival or departure from the hospital, I remarked to one of the European staff how incongruous it was to wear fur hats in the summer in a hot climate. The hat wearers themselves were unwilling to reveal the reasons for their unusual headdress until it was reported in the press that in future the wearing of fur hats was to be banned because it had been adopted as a nationalist emblem.

It was at this time that trouble flared up in the Belgian Congo, until then considered to be an impeccable example of colonial administration. I describe earlier how a white resident in the Congo had criticized British colonial development for being too slow. The Congo administration had taken a far more active role in educating and advancing its indigenous population and, unlike its federal counterpart, had allowed Africans to engage in skilled occupations, such as driving passenger trains. It seemed ironic that in 1960 and for no apparent reason the Belgian government should hand over the territory to African nationalists. In a short while there was chaos in the country. The army revolted and violence and looting broke out in Elizabethville, the modern and prosperous capital of Katanga Province close to the Northern Rhodesian border. The Europeans had to flee for their lives to neighbouring countries and thousands came over the border into Northern Rhodesia in a great hurry. They arrived in cars, trucks and even farm tractors. One refugee drove over in a fire engine. Most of them carried on into Southern Rhodesia, and Salisbury was inundated with thousands of refugees. The city council made special arrangements to feed and accommodate them — in the agricultural-show grounds and in private residences. They were eventually repatriated to Belgium by the Belgian government. Not surprisingly, the Congo debacle made the European residents in Rhodesia think and worry about their own future.

Because of the Southern Rhodesian government's insistence on independence, a new constitution was negotiated with the British government. The electorate was asked to vote in a referendum for its acceptance. Under the new 1961 constitution the British government gave up its reserve powers, but it included a bill of rights for all races and improved the Africans' franchise and representation in parliament. We voted for acceptance of the new constitution and were surprised that a large majority of the electorate, about two to one, voted in its favour. It was rejected by the Dominion Party because it was too pro-African, and by Africans, who did not vote in the referendum, because they wanted a 'one man one vote' constitution and would accept nothing less.

I found it difficult to contemplate the significance of race relations in Southern Rhodesia in the early 1960s. The range of

European attitudes was very wide — from Afrikaans bigots who did not consider blacks worthy of being described as human beings to university lecturers and students who accepted Africans as equals and treated them as such. Some joined African nationalist political parties and socialized with blacks, but the vast majority of Europeans looked upon Africans, who were still predominantly employed in menial or unskilled jobs, as ignorant toiling hoi polloi. The average European only came into contact with Africans as master and servant or as an employer of labour.

My own position was different; the nature of my employment necessitated being in contact with Africans most of the working day and I had ample opportunity to learn about their cultural, social and economic background. I took the trouble to learn Shona, the language spoken by the people of Mashonaland, which is in the northern part of Southern Rhodesia, where we lived. In evening classes at the local polytechnic we concentrated on one of the four dialects used in Mashonaland, the local dialect known as Zezuru.

Shona is a highly complex language; it has a written grammar and is rich in the description of natural fauna. Modern words are mostly onomatopoeic. For example a telephone is called a 'telephono', a railway engine a 'sithema', and an aeroplane a 'fly-machine'. I found the Shona people pleasant, easy going, co-operative and undemonstrative. They have a keen sense of humour and tend to be fatalistic, which became noticeable when treating them as patients. They found it difficult to answer a question with a reply they did not think would please the questioner.

Having acquired a modicum of Zezuru, it was instructive and amusing being able to follow Africans' conversations. On one occasion I heard a white visitor from South Africa, who was having his car filled with petrol in front of me at a garage in Salisbury, greet the African attendant with the usual, 'Good morning boy. How are things with you up here'? His reply in English of, 'Fine Sir. Everything is fine here,' was followed by an aside to another African employee standing nearby of, 'Listen to this stupid white man asking me silly questions!'

White people addressed all African men as 'boy', irrespective of how young or old they appeared to be. Africans were invariably courteous in their greetings to each other. For example, whereas we greet each other in the early morning with a curt, 'Good morning', with a similar reply, the African greeting is more elaborate — 'Good morning and how did you sleep?' The reply to this would be, 'I slept well provided I know that you slept well,' and then finally 'I slept well'. There is a different form of greeting for later in the morning. The nomenclature used by the different races in Southern Rhodesia to describe each other was complicated, but instructive with regard to race relations. All blacks were officially designated as NATIVES. All whites were officially called EUROPEANS, whether or not they had been born in the country; a Rhodesian-born white citizen was not referred to as a native. Other large groups, such as Indians, were officially called ASIATICS, and those of mixed race COLOUREDS.

Europeans, when not using official language, usually called a black man a *munt*, but a black female would be called a native girl or woman and occasionally would be referred to as a nanny. The word *munt* was derived from the Shona name for a man or person, which is *munhu*. The word *munt* was not used in a derogatory sense, but I would describe it as disrespectful. Working-class Europeans often called a black person a *coon*, which I would define as a derogatory description. More race conscious South Africans living in Southern Rhodesia and known as Afrikaners, would often refer to a black person as a *kaffir*, which literally means a disbeliever, but was used in a derogatory sense by the Afrikaners. The African name for a European was *umshlungu* (in phonetic spelling), but returning the compliment referred to an Afrikaner as a *mabora*, an uncomplimentary name derived from the word *boer*, the Afrikaans word for a farmer. It will be noted that throughout this treatise I have always referred to a black person as an African which is the official term used to describe such a person in Northern Rhodesia. When we were resident there we became used to this description, which we regarded as the most satisfactory designation.

At times Africans could be annoying merely because they lacked so-called European sophistication. Many European settlers, especially females, described their black servants as lazy, stupid and unclean. In my experience many white females had a pathological hatred of blacks. There was a junior typist in my office, whose window overlooked the bus terminus down below, where an African inspector and several drivers often congregated. This young lady spent most of her time calling them offensive names. They were not noisy and there was no reason why she should be so antagonistic to them without any evident cause. She was Rhodesian-born and I asked her on a number of occasions why she hated blacks so much. It has been suggested that such unjustifiable hatred of blacks is sexual in origin, but I do not accept this pseudo-analytical explanation.

I was attending a well-publicized meeting addressed by a delegation of Europeans from Northern Rhodesia, when it soon became apparent that the purpose of the meeting was to seek support in Southern Rhodesia for these delegates' futile and ridiculous opposition to rising African political demands in their country. The delegates, whom I recognized as politicians and businessmen, suggested and demanded that Kenneth Kaunda, the leader of the African nationalist party, should be detained and put behind bars! Like all leaders of political opposition in British colonial territories, he was eventually so detained.

I am unable to recollect exactly when during our stay in Salisbury the following experience occurred, but it is one I find difficult to forget. We arose as usual to the sound of the early morning radio news bulletin. It included a report of unrest and rioting in Harare, the largest African township in the Salisbury area, but as reports of unrest in an African township were not unusual, it was soon forgotten. This was a day when I visited the large municipal clinic in Harare to see any cases referred to me by the sister-in-charge.

When I arrived at the entrance to the township I noticed large numbers of European and African policemen lying exhausted on the grass verge alongside the road. This jogged my memory of the news about rioting in the township. It was about 9.00 a.m. and the European sister would have arrived at the clinic at about 8.30 a.m. I enquired from the police if the sister had gone through into the township, but they were so exhausted that their reply was inconclusive. Without thinking or realizing how irrational I was being, I instinctively drove along the straight road into the township to the clinic, which was about a quarter of a mile along the road and surrounded by a garden. I entered the drive and parked as usual in front of the clinic.

As I got out of the car I sensed a queer, low-toned, eerie buzzing in the air. I had read about the 'air being electric' and thought that this was an apt description. On entering the clinic the four medical orderlies, all Nyasas, came out to greet me. Their eyes were bloodshot and they were very agitated. The senior orderly told me that they had been up all night and that no patients had attended the clinic that morning because of rioting and tear gas in the vicinity. They were concerned about me having come to the clinic because, as they said, it was very dangerous for a European to be there and I could easily be killed. They implored me to leave immediately.

I then realized that I had unintentionally placed myself in an invidious position. I thought of phoning the police for help, but then realized that the phone lines would probably have been cut. Putting on a brave front, I slowly returned to my car and drove away on the same road by which I had entered the township a short while before. I had proceeded about 100 yards when a crowd of Africans appeared on the road. As I was slowly negotiating my way past them, they started to bang the car with their fists. Then a rock came through the open window next to the driver's seat, just missed my neck and landed on the floor of the car. This was soon followed by a barrage of rocks. The back and rear car windows were smashed and a small rock hit my arm. I eventually managed to get back to the police lines. It was only then that I realized I had driven back in second gear lying across the front seat using the roofs of the double-storeyed hostels along the length of the road as my guide. There were a number of dents in the bodywork of my recently purchased car.

The sister had wisely refrained from entering the township. What upset me most about the episode was the council's response when I asked them to pay for the extensive repairs to my car. They advised me to apply to a special charity set up for the purpose of meeting any expenses incurred as a result of damage done by African terrorists or rioters. I flatly refused on the grounds that the damage was done while I was on duty and the council should have advised all European employees not to enter Harare township on the day in question. They loaned me a municipal car and eventually paid for the repairs to my car. It was only natural that I was not well disposed to African nationalists for the time being.

Shortly before this episode our cook joined the auxiliary police. We were pleased about this, for it gave us a sense of security. He was issued with a dark blue uniform and hat and, on three nights a week, would go out on patrol from the local police station. Once again the idiocy of repressive legislation was exemplified when an African was charged and fined £25 for calling these special constables girl guides!

While motoring through the city centre one day I came across some territorial soldiers enthusiastically sacking the headquarters of ZAPU (Zimbabwe African People's Union) and ripping its signs and emblems from the side of the building. This followed the banning of the party and the detention of its president, Joshua Nkomo. ZAPU was the third African nationalist party to be banned and we were to hear a lot more about its leader in the future. African youth leagues continued to be active in the townships, intimidating residents who joined European political parties or exercised their vote in an election. Up to this juncture, most of the violence was confined to blacks — whites were rarely involved.

Despite the occasional upset, life continued to be very pleasant and relaxed in Salisbury. For Europeans these were still halcyon days. In later years an author described his life in Salisbury during this period as being in Shangri-la.

Nevertheless, there was a perceptible change in attitudes. The activities of the Mau Mau in Kenya and the Congo debacle had made white Rhodesians more conscious of their vulnerability. We began to realize that black Rhodesians were no longer willing to cooperate with European political movements to achieve their aspiration of 'one man one vote'. They preferred to progress through their own political activity. As a result, European thought and political activity became increasingly reactionary. Africans were becoming more confident of winning their struggle to obtain political power in a much shorter timescale than that envisaged by the whites. The European sister in charge of the Harare township

121

clinic told me that three, pleasant, middle-aged Africans had visited the clinic and officially informed her that she would be acceptable to the African government when it came into power because she worked with and was kind to Africans.

* * *

In retrospect 1962 was a momentous year because the United Federal Party government under Whitehead had been in power for four years and a general election was due to be held. It was also a year of profound political change in the country. There were only two important parties to contest the election, the ruling United Federal Party and the Dominion Party.

On reflection, the Dominion Party, which was known to be right-wing, did not appear to have a large following or much influence in the early part of the year. It included some incomprehensible contradictions. Dr Ahrn Palley, who was a personal friend of mine and who had deserted the medical profession to become a dedicated pro-African politician, joined the party. When asked why he had decided to support this reactionary bunch, he gave a tactical political explanation we were unable to understand. It was also rumoured that Sir Robert Tredgold, the former chief justice, had given the party his blessing.

It was decided that the general election would be held at the end of the year. In the meantime, Dominion Party candidates constantly criticized the government because they considered that it was too liberal and should be adopting more oppressive measures against the black nationalists. The United Federal Party under Whitehead had genuinely tried to carry out a policy of partnership between the races and openly stated that it was its intention to repeal the Land Apportionment Act, which formed the basis of the demarcation of the territory into separate areas for whites and blacks and, in practice, was similar to the apartheid system in South Africa. There was increasing opposition to its progressive programme and one frequently heard anti-government opinions expressed by friends and acquaintances who should have known better.

The Dominion Party kept on changing its leaders. A name often mentioned in the media as a financial supporter of the party was a prosperous farmer by the name of 'Boss' Lilford. He had considerable influence in the party and was reputed to be a rabid negrophobe. When a black government came into power many years later, he was one of the first autocrats to be liquidated. The party eventually appointed Mr Winston Field, a pleasant, popular former federal member of parliament who commanded respect, as its new leader. He brought prestige to the party, which in the meantime had changed its name to the Rhodesian Front. Under Winston Field's leadership, the Rhodesian Front gradually gained support and influence.

Later in the year a young man visited our residence and invited us to a political meeting at the home of a dentist who lived nearby but whom we had never met. He admitted that this private gathering was to be held in support of the Rhodesian Front. We did not trouble to attend. Then shortly afterwards we were phoned by a friend who owned a luxurious residence and property to which we had frequently been invited to tennis and swimming parties. Once again I was invited to attend a political meeting at his abode. Under the circumstances I found it difficult to refuse and turned up at the meeting in due course. There were about 15 well-heeled local residents present at the gathering. As was to be expected, they were all European. After a while I felt out of place because it became apparent to me that I was the only unenthusiastic member of the audience; all those who spoke were critical of the government, which was far too liberal for their liking. They feared that unless the present government were replaced by a more counter-revolutionary regime, a black government would take over power in the not too distant future. One member of the meeting, whom I later discovered was a prosperous businessman, spoke with a pronounced South African accent. He referred to the blacks as 'Kaffirs' and was violent in his belief that they should be dealt with in a bloodthirsty manner.

Before the election, which was held in December, and despite all the private political activity on behalf of the Rhodesian Front, we were confident that the UFP would be re-elected by a large majority. One had to take account of the fact that it was a direct

123

descendant of the old Huggins' party, which had been in power since 1933. Furthermore, it had been supported by a two to one majority in the 1961 constitutional referendum which advocated a more progressive government. It represented the establishment, had the support of black voters, and the approval of Sir Roy Welensky and Lord Malvern.

Like most other citizens, we were surprised and shocked when we heard the result of the election. The RF had won by a comfortable majority. The Africans, who had been advised by their nationalist leaders to boycott the election, in the main did not register their votes. They were not unduly worried about the election result because they now believed that no European minority government would willingly transfer power to a black government, despite all their talk about partnership. Dr Ahrn Palley was elected as an independent in a non-European constituency. Another surprising result was that the majority of Coloureds and Asiatics had voted in favour of the RF. As a community they were uncertain where they belonged, but apparently considered their interests were with the European minority rather than with the African majority.

Shortly after the general election in Southern Rhodesia, the British government decided that Nyasaland should be allowed to secede from the federation. This made Welensky even more vehement in his condemnation of the British government and politicians, for he wished to preserve the union between the Rhodesias on economic grounds. By this time the majority of white Rhodesians had given up their hopes about the future of the federation. The new RF government, under the leadership of Winston Field, openly stated that it did not support the federation.

Rhodesia was a very British-oriented territory and in some respects was more English than England. The majority of residents in the suburb in which we lived in Salisbury were from England or had English connections. It was similar to an English village with its local C of E church. Many people still spoke of England as 'home' and, like ourselves, continued to spend their leave or holidays in the United Kingdom. The majority of cars on the roads were manufactured in England and the only motorcar assembly plant in Rhodesia was owned by the British Motor Corporation.

At about this time opinions were changing. Welensky's tirades against the British government and its ministers began to rub off onto the European populace. Britain's overt interest in the advancement of Africans, its refusal to grant Southern Rhodesia complete sovereignty, and Duncan Sandys's statement that 'Britain had lost the will to govern in her African colonial possessions' resulted in an anti-British attitude becoming discernible.

For the next 18 months the Field government continued to administer the country in an acceptable manner. Economic progress in the manufacturing sector and agricultural output, especially of tobacco, were impressive. Apart from the white typists with whom I came into daily contact becoming increasingly offensive and bigoted towards blacks, I experienced no problems in my professional or administrative work. Our social lives were unaffected, though Europeans were gradually becoming more fearful of their underprivileged black countrymen,.

During his period as prime minister we met Mr Winston Field on two occasions, both at open days at the public school his and our sons attended. On both occasions he was accompanied by a large Alsatian dog, which the police loaned to him as a bodyguard on the understanding that he would not go outdoors unaccompanied by the hound. We found him to be a pleasant, moderate English gentleman who had immigrated to Rhodesia to become a farmer. He was so different from the usual extroverted, slick politician that we wondered why he had ever become a legislator. We did not agree with his political policies, and I remember how, in a speech, he had blamed the United Nations, Great Britain and other outside influences for the racial unrest in Rhodesia. Despite his reactionary outlook he was a comparatively moderate leader and was not a racist.

Following the example of Nyasaland, under the leadership of Kenneth Kaunda, president of the United National Independence Party, the Northern Rhodesian Africans increased their agitation to secede from the federation and be granted independence under their own government. The British government had little alternative but to agree to their demand. This was a deathblow for the Central African Federation, which was dismantled at the end of 1963. A conference was arranged to meet at the Victoria Falls to

discuss the 'orderly dissolution of the federation'. All five governments concerned were represented at the conference under the
chairmanship of Mr Rab Butler, whom Prime Minister Macmillan
had appointed as the minister in charge of Central African affairs.
Welensky described him as 'an undertaker who had come to bury
the corpse'. The deliberations at the conference were unexpectedly
amicable. Problems such as splitting up the railways and other
federal consortiums were overcome without difficulty. With the
dismantling of the federation, Nyasaland became Malawi, with Dr
Hastings Banda as president, and Northern Rhodesia became
Zambia, with Kenneth Kaunda as president. Sir Roy Welensky
decided to retire from politics.

With the demise of the federation, Winston Field and his
government took it for granted that Southern Rhodesia, now to be
known as Rhodesia, would be given sovereign independence.
However, this did not eventuate.

On recollection, it was not easy for the British government to
grant Rhodesia complete independence in the Commonwealth for
a number of reasons. Such a move would have been open to
criticism or condemnation from various international bodies such
as the United Nations and the Commonwealth but, more important, British public opinion had become more progressive and
tolerant; giving in to the European settler demands in Rhodesia
would have been unacceptable.

Following its defeat by the RF in the 1962 general election, the
UFP had become demoralized. Still under the leadership of
Whitehead, it did not make an effective opposition in the Legislative Assembly and the pro-African Dr Ahrn Palley emerged as the
main opposition parliamentarian.

The African nationalist movement had split. Mr Joshua Nkomo,
the leader of ZAPU, had been condemned for his over tolerant
approach in their struggle for political power and a new party,
ZANU (Zimbabwe African Nationalist Union), was formed. In the
course of time Mr Field's popularity began to decline. His leadership was blamed because independence had not been granted and
African nationalism had been compromised.

The racial extremists in the RF began to get restless and became
critical of Mr Field. He was too much of a gentleman to challenge

them openly in public and, towards the middle of 1964, he decided
to resign as prime minister. We thought he had been pushed out by
the extreme right wingers in his party. He was replaced by Mr Ian
Smith.

* * *

Ian Smith was a totally different character from Winston Field. He
was a narrow-minded, idealistic bigot who thought he had the
answer to all Rhodesia's problems. His over-simplified solution
was to obtain independence from the UK by fair means or foul and
to keep the blacks in their place. Shortly after becoming prime
minister he disclosed his intentions by saying that 'the blacks will
not take over power in my lifetime', and he was a comparatively
young man! He further made it known that if independence were
not granted by negotiation in a reasonable time it would have to
be taken unconstitutionally.

It was not long before leading African nationalists were once
again being incarcerated. Nationalist activities were constrained to
such an extent that a few of the leaders (those who managed to
escape) transferred their party headquarters to adjacent territories
that had already been granted independence. ZAPU went to
Lusaka in Zambia and ZANU to Dar es Salaam in Tanzania.

Rhodesia had now become a police state. Smith and his cronies
endeavoured to persuade all whites to support their programme
and refused to accept any criticism. An obnoxious young South
African immigrant by the name of van der Byl was chosen to be
the minister of information.

He immediately launched into an attack on the press, which was
owned by the South African Argus Group and up to then had
supported the UFP through its two main publications, the
Salisbury Herald and the *Bulawayo Chronicle*. These were liberal
newspapers and the only two dailies with a wide European
circulation. Another daily paper, the *Daily News*, owned by the
Thompson Group in the UK, had a wide African readership and
reported their nationalist activities. Though a serious newspaper
that did not indulge in any brainwashing, it was banned shortly

after Smith's government came to power. Van der Byl intimidated the Argus Group's journalists and warned them against publishing any opinions other than those that supported the views of the Rhodesian Front.

The government decided to appoint a South African expert on right-wing propaganda to work in its so-called Information Department. His name was Ivor Benson and it was said that South Africa was pleased to get rid of him because his views were too reactionary, even for their liking. His vitriolic tirades over the radio and on television against communists, the United Nations, the Church and Africans reminded me of Goebbels, the Nazi minister of information. The government began to use the radio and television as vehicles for the dissemination of official propaganda.

My eldest son was in his third year at the university, which granted University of London degrees. A number of the lecturers and students became very concerned by the trend of events and on the day it was announced that the banning of the *Daily News* was to be debated in Parliament, they decided to organize a peaceful demonstration outside the House of Assembly. When the students gathered there that afternoon the police immediately ordered them to disperse. They did not go away, but sat down in an empty area opposite the House of Assembly displaying copies of the *Daily News*, which that day carried large headlines supporting non-violence! They were silent and did not cause an obstruction, but the police arrived in force in police vehicles and arrested them all. The students were transported to the central police station and locked up in overcrowded cells, significantly separated by sex but not colour. The majority, about 90 of them, went on trial a few weeks later, but were discharged because identification of all the accused was not possible.

Three students, Judy Todd, the daughter of the previous prime minister Garfield Todd, a black student by the name of Byron Hove, who eventually became a leading advocate in Salisbury, and my son were charged at a separate trial because they were designated as ringleaders. Garfield Todd and I attended the trial from beginning to end. Police informers amongst the students at the university (Rhodesian Front supporters) stated that Judy Todd,

Hove and my son had originally suggested the demonstration at breakfast on the actual day on which it was held. The police evidence at the trial was contradictory and ridiculous, but the magistrate gave the impression, by his manner and attitude, that this was a purely political case and that he had been instructed to find the accused guilty, despite there being no evidence to prove their guilt. They were each fined £25, which was paid from a collection organized among their fellow students.

It was about this time that Smith addressed a public meeting in the Athenium Hall, a Greek amenity in Salisbury. The meeting was well advertised and I decided to attend it purely out of curiosity. The hall was already packed by the time I arrived, but I somehow managed to obtain a seat near the back. The hall was decorated with flags and a blown-up photograph of Smith adorned the back of the platform. There were a few Africans in the audience. Smith strode in with a retinue of followers and walked onto the stage like a tinpot dictator attempting to emulate more famous despots in Europe who had since met their just fates. The audience rose to welcome him. I then noticed a row of students in the middle of the hall who remained seated; I became extremely worried when I saw that both my sons and other students whom I knew were among them. Some of the students heckled Smith when he made his stock remarks about independence and maintaining civilized standards. A government minister on the platform dared the students to stand up and be seen. They did this without hesitation and I admired their pluck. Members of the audience immediately attacked the students and pushed them back into their seats and onto the floor. Smith and his cronies looked on the scene with satisfaction and made no attempt to persuade the attackers to desist. The students were eventually rescued by detectives and policemen who escorted them out of the hall and back to the university. A distressed middle-aged woman wept outside the hall after the meeting. She was a German refugee who said that the meeting had reminded her of the Hitler era in Germany.

To my mind Rhodesia now had an authoritarian government with a fascist attitude. I use the word fascist advisedly because, with its control of information and refusal to accept any criticism, the government exhibited all the trappings of an anti-communist fascist state. The police and army were ruthless in their treatment of black citizens. I actually witnessed police in Harare wake all the residents in a large area of the township one night and line them up outside while their homes were searched for dissidents. Despite increasing rumours of government plans to use unconstitutional measures to obtain independence, Smith continued to negotiate with the British government and denied he had any intention of acting unconstitutionally. Smith himself made a poor dictator. He was not nearly as relentless as many of his followers. These included the South Africans, van der Byl and Lardner Burke, various renegade Englishmen, including a noble lord, and a former district commissioner in Northern Rhodesia by the name of Gaunt, an extreme right-wing fanatic, who came up with brutal suggestions for dealing with African nationalists. I had heard adverse criticism of him when we lived in Livingstone. He was the 'bad apple in the barrel' as far as the provincial administration in Northern Rhodesia was concerned. He eventually became too extreme even for Smith, who got rid of him by appointing him Rhodesian ambassador in South Africa. The opposition in Parliament had become unsettled and its condemnation of the government was perfunctory and ineffective.

By now the Europeans had formed themselves into a white laager surrounded by blacks. There was increasing acceptance of the ideas expressed by the Rhodesian Front. 'The granting of independence' and 'the maintenance of civilized standards' became emotional clichés. Uninformed political discussion became fashionable and the idea of a Unilateral Declaration of Independence was frequently expressed. You either supported the Rhodesian Front and the government, which had become indistinguishable, or you were a communist. There was nothing in between and it was becoming increasingly difficult to remain open-minded in such a reactionary society. We became estranged from many of our friends because of our different political opinions. We even knew people whose families split up over political issues, which created considerable bad feeling and unhappiness. On the few occasions I was called a communist to my face, I calmly asked whether they thought I was a Trotskyist or a Stalinist. Without exception my denouncers looked blank and failed to answer my question. My wife was a very keen bridge player, but the situation had got so bad that she found it necessary before a game commenced to inform the other players that 'they may or may not know her views, but she had come to enjoy a game of bridge and if there was any political discussion she would immediately stop playing and go home'. This ploy was successful in preventing acrimonious arguments.

My friend Jock Anderson, a fine, intelligent, broad-minded general who commanded the troops in the Rhodesian Army, did not disguise his political views. In fact he publicly stated that he would not support a government that contemplated unconstitutional action. He was retired in October 1964 on the 'grounds of old age' when he was in his early fifties. He privately informed me that he thought the RF was prepared to take the Africans on in military combat, despite his advice to the contrary. He said it would take up to 100 men to find and destroy a determined gunman armed with a kalashnikov sub-machine-gun in the bush. He told me he intended to leave Rhodesia for the sake of his two teenage sons who could become involved in a racial war in the future. Because the blacks outnumbered the whites by over 20 to one, it was inconceivable that the whites would be victorious. I also had two teenage sons and readily accepted the implication of his warning.

The African nationalist leaders were all either in detention or in some way restricted. New draconian laws had been introduced to allow suspects to be arrested and detained without trial. Though African political activity was subdued in the territory, ZANU and ZAPU continued to function in exile in Tanzania and Zambia. Government propaganda continually proclaimed that the chiefs in the African reserves were the true leaders of the African people. They may have had tribal authority in the 'sticks', but in reality they were civil servants who were paid by the state and who supported the government. If a chief had the temerity to disagree with government policy he was soon sacked. Most articulate Africans were detribalized and lived in towns, so they did not accept the authority of the chiefs.

This was another example of the government using dishonest propaganda to achieve their own wicked objectives. Despite all the

131

dubious political changes, my work as a local government employee was not affected. I was not unduly worried by the mounting animosity of a doctor and several half-witted office employees who regarded me as a dissident.

Europeans who were critical of the government were few and far between and instinctively gravitated towards one another at functions or on social occasions. We eventually formed a loose alliance of like-minded moderates who met at each other's houses for Sunday morning drinks. There were about 40 regular participants.

I look back on these gatherings with gratitude because they helped overcome the distress of being political and social outcasts. There were no politicians or political activists among us. Neither were there any African participants, not because this was intentional, but because, under the Group Areas Act, Africans were obliged to live in prescribed areas of the city. Also, it is doubtful that many Africans would have acquired the sophistication to be interested in our group, which included a well-known British banker and a Lord of the Realm. Visiting overseas politicians were invited to address our gatherings. One such example was Jeremy Thorpe, the then leader of the British Liberal Party. I also recollect a British Labour Party politician, the bearded actor Andrew Faulds, rather forcibly express the opinion that we did not really oppose Smith's government because we were not active enough to be detained in gaol as a political protest. I personally accepted his advice with reservations.

In the stifling atmosphere of an authoritarian state, it was another consolation to be able to drive from Salisbury to Beira (in adjoining Mozambique) between an early breakfast and late lunch. Besides being an important port for the import and export of goods (essential for the Rhodesian economy), Beira was a pleasant, rather continental seaside resort with a large sandy beach and excellent sunbathing facilities. Good Portuguese wines, local beers and shellfish, such as lobster and jumbo prawns, were plentiful and cheap. We had several enjoyable short breaks there. Though overall the Portuguese were no more successful as colonists than the British, there was far more racial integration in Mozambique than in Rhodesia. Blacks and whites could be seen socializing and dancing together at the best hotels and nightclubs. The Portuguese handed the territory over to President Machel, a professed communist, in 1974 — much to the consternation of the Smith government in the adjacent territory.

Soon after we settled in Salisbury, I visited an old army friend who introduced me to a tall, imposing man who was leaving as I arrived. His name was 'Tiny' Rowland. As he drove off, my friend said that his departing guest had grand ideas and would be a millionaire or in gaol within the next two years. The former turned out to be the true prediction. He became chairman of Lonrho, a Rhodesian mining and farming company, and turned it into a company of worldwide repute. It had large successful business enterprises in Central Africa. One of his ideas, which he managed to achieve, was to build an oil pipeline from Beira to the Rhodesian border town of Umtali.

As negotiations about independence between the Rhodesian and British governments dragged on, more talk was heard about taking unconstitutional means to achieve it. The drastic consequences of a Unilateral Declaration of Independence (UDI) were communicated to Smith by the British prime minister, Sir Alec Douglas-Home, and later by Harold Wilson, who became prime minister following the Labour Party's victory. He was warned that Rhodesia would be cut off from the United Kingdom and the Commonwealth, that it would not be internationally recognized, that it would suffer unfavourable economic relations and that sanctions would most probably be applied. Local farming, commercial and industrial organizations all pointed out that their interests would be adversely affected if unlawful means were adopted to obtain independence. Smith and his ministers ignored these warnings and confused the issue by insisting, on flimsy grounds, that the country could only benefit from attaining independence, even if by unlawful means. They argued that Rhodesia had not suffered economic decline, as had been predicted, following the break-up of the federation. Smith said it would merely amount to a 'three day wonder' in the City of London.

At about this time the electorate was invited to vote in a referendum on some political subterfuge to give the RF more support. As expected, those in favour of the RF outnumbered those against by a majority of ten to one. We did not take the trouble to vote. Dissent was now treasonable and support for the government even more intense. As I mention earlier, this was difficult to understand because, to all intents and purposes, Rhodesia had been independent since 1923. The present governor was a Rhodesian and the United Kingdom was represented by a high commissioner. Why the average citizen should be emotionally worried about complete sovereignty was beyond our comprehension. The cry to maintain so-called 'civilized standards' was more understandable because it was an apocryphal behest to maintain their superior, comfortable way of life by exploiting the blacks.

Another general election was held in 1965. My wife and I tried, with all our powers of persuasion, to implore our friends and acquaintances not to vote for the RF because its policies would eventually lead to a racial war. And, as we were outnumbered by more than 20 to one, the Europeans were bound to be defeated and their husbands and sons killed or maimed in what would inevitably amount to a bush war. A not unexpected reply from a European male would be, 'I am equal to at least 100 *munt*s, so there is no need to worry on that score.'

When the results of the election were announced we were flabbergasted. They had voted like a flock of turkeys voting for Christmas — the Smith government had won all the European seats. The opposition now consisted of about ten Africans who had won separate role votes in district seats and the indomitable Dr Palley, who had also won a district seat as an independent. The official European opposition was eliminated. Very few of the Africans who were entitled to vote supported the election.

Following the election, which showed that Smith had the complete European support he desired, UDI seemed inevitable. However, negotiations continued but no satisfactory solution was found. In desperation, Harold Wilson came to Rhodesia and we hoped something would come about as a result of this unexpected development. He interviewed the detained African nationalist leaders as well as members of the government. On his return to England it transpired that no agreement had been made. A few weeks later, in a lunch-time news bulletin on Armistice Day, 11 November 1965, Smith announced his Unilateral Declaration of

Independence. After hearing Smith's boring, toneless voice announce the UDI we felt completely desolate. It is difficult to explain in words how we felt after the announcement, but it was rather like knowing that someone is going to die, but nevertheless being shocked when death finally occurs. Of course this was a personal reaction and we imagined that the vast majority of Europeans welcomed the announcement.

I returned to my office following the lunch break and was unhappy to see that there was a noisy party going on. I was offered a glass of sparkling wine, which I refused. I then openly told them that this was not the time to rejoice, but to wear sackcloth and ashes. Despite my request to the office staff, a number of health inspectors, and one of the medical officers to get back to work as it was after the end of the lunch break, I was ignored and the party continued. In desperation I told them they were misguided morons, put on my jacket and departed for home. I later learned that no further work was done in the office that day.

After UDI, the situation quickly deteriorated. Press censorship was introduced and blank white spaces began to appear in the newspapers where censors had objected to a news item being published. The Rhodesian public was shielded from any criticism of the government, and from any information that was in way complimentary to adjoining African states that had already become independent. Van der Byl and his hireling, Benson, used the radio and television for their anti-communist, pro-government propaganda. Literature was also subjected to censorship and books containing any suggestion of liberal thought were banned.

The absence of reliable local and overseas news gave us a feeling of mental claustrophobia and we have to thank the BBC for its news programme entitled 'The World and Rhodesia', which was broadcast from Botswana, close to the Rhodesian border, at midday each day. For some reason reception of the programme was distorted when attempting to receive it through an ordinary radio set, most likely due to jamming, but it could be heard clearly on the radio in my car. No matter where I was or what I was doing I did not miss the daily broadcast, which was our only reliable source of world and local news. In retrospect life would have been unbearable without this daily injection of factual information; it helped keep up our spirits and morale.

The nauseating propaganda now being disseminated, together with the ruthless repression of the African population, amounted to a reign of terror to keep the ruling whites in power. Smith and his gang of right-wing politicians were morally bankrupt and clearly indulging in prevarication. It is inconceivable that they did not know that their repeated claims that African political opinion could be obtained from the chiefs were untrue. The British government never accepted this line and, in any case, the chiefs were mostly too ignorant to understand the significance of political thinking or intention. The government's fatuous remarks about Rhodesia being the last country to preserve decency and Christianity in a decadent world and the last bulwark against the spread of world communism, were arrogant nonsense. It was all reminiscent of Nazi propaganda in Germany before and during the Second World War.

A state of emergency had been instituted by the governor, Sir Humphrey Gibbs, a few days before UDI. Lardner Burke, the so-called minister of justice, had authoritative power to restrict or detain any person under the Law and Order Maintenance Act. He had been my personal solicitor in Gwelo and it is not easy to understand how this pleasant lawyer, whom I had known many years previously, had become an ogre to those who did not support Smith's government. It was always difficult to comprehend how many of our friends and acquaintances changed from being moderate in their political views to becoming ardent supporters of the Rhodesian Front's reactionary government. Soon after UDI Mr Ben Baron, a lawyer I had known in Northern Rhodesia, who was a well-known legal adviser to some of the African nationalist leaders, was imprisoned and eventually deported.

We were sent printed air-mail propaganda letters issued by the government with a request to forward them to families or friends overseas. The letter stated, 'Rhodesia is a peaceful country in which there is little friction between the races, and most Rhodesians, black and white, are contented and happy.' Needless to say we refrained from sending any of these lying epistles to any unsuspecting individuals who lived abroad.

The governor, Sir Humphrey Gibbs, was requested to vacate Government House in Salisbury, where they intended to install their new president. Sir Humphrey refused to leave and pro-British individuals like ourselves, who were antagonistic to UDI, paid into a fund each month to maintain the governor in his rightful place. The Smith government took away his official car, which was given to its president for his official use, and threatened to cut off the water supply to Government House, which our department managed to prevent on health grounds. All official guards and Government House staff were removed on the day following UDI. We visited Government House on the queen's birthday to sign 'the book'. An obnoxious BSAP constable stood by and was overtly rude to those of us who came to sign the book. Sir Humphrey maintained his dignity during those difficult days, but we were disappointed that he continued to visit the Salisbury Club where he came into contact with leading RF supporters. He had been a farmer in Matabeleland before his appointment as the governor general of Rhodesia.

It was noteworthy that the African population remained reticent following UDI and I cannot recall any instance in which I ever discussed the matter with an African acquaintance. The reason for the African taciturnity and lack of action, which was criticized by some other liberated African states, was multifactorial. The African nationalist opposition was split — most of its leaders were detained in custody or were in exile — and constant harassment by the police and army had demoralized the African population and those leaders who remained at large. The only occasion when the African opposition did unite was about a year previously when the government decided that Africans would have to pay for their children's education while European children continued to enjoy free education. They did not unite to protest against UDI. We learned later that, like us, African opinion thought that the United Kingdom would not accept the declaration without more overt protest. We even believed that military force would be used, but it was openly stated that the British policy was not to use force. As one Zambian politician appropriately remarked, 'The British lion has lost its teeth.' In any case, with the passage of time I gained the impression that the blacks most likely considered this to be a

European problem and that their predicament could not be made worse by the UDI. As was to be expected, African reticence was used as a propaganda manoeuvre by the government, which publicized their relative silence as a sign of their acceptance of UDI.

The United Kingdom was slow to come to terms with its mutinous colony. Its advice to all Rhodesians, shortly after UDI, was to stay at their posts and keep working as usual. This was to apply especially to the police, members of the armed forces and the civil service, in order to prevent chaos. The day following the UDI I had to visit the American library and reading room in Salisbury to refer urgently to some papers with regard to my work. When I arrived the doors were closed and locked. A notice stated that they would be closed until further notice. Some days later the British Council closed its doors. At this time I was attending lectures on the Shona language and one of the other students was a BOAC employee. The airline did not close the shop it occupied in the centre of the city and she informed me that they had not been notified that they would close. The only aircraft landing in Rhodesia, other than local Rhodesian craft, were South African or Portuguese owned. Throughout the period of the rebellion it was possible to book a BOAC flight to any destination overseas. Rhodesian or South African aircraft would be used to fly to Johannesburg and then the passengers would transfer to a BOAC aircraft for the flight to London. I thought this was a prima-facie case of breaking their own sanctions, which were to be used as the United Kingdom's main weapon in bringing down the Smith government. This was apparently approved by the United Nations; it was not until mid-1968 that mandatory sanctions were imposed against Rhodesia by the UN Security Council.

The main objective of sanctions at the time was to prevent the delivery of petroleum products into Rhodesia. Apparently the British lion had not lost all its teeth because it was reported that British warships and submarines were patrolling the Indian Ocean to prevent the passage of oil tankers into the port of Beira, from where oil could be pumped through the Lonrho pipeline into Rhodesia. This, however, did not prevent the delivery of petrol into Rhodesia by road tankers from South Africa. We were all aware of the evasion of sanctions at the time. There was a story going around about how a well-groomed British civil servant with a bowler hat and rolled umbrella had been seen taking down the numbers of petrol tankers as they crossed the border into Rhodesia! It was derisive that it took a judicial inquiry (the Bingham Report) in the United Kingdom many years later to show that the petrol sanctions had been a farce. We could have told them at the time that British oil companies were openly breaking sanctions, which were only applied half heartedly. It is interesting to note that Conservatives in England objected to sanctions being imposed against Rhodesia because they would harm the blacks more than the whites. This was the very same argument used more recently against the imposition of sanctions against South Africa, a case of history repeating itself. Looking out of my office window I had a clear view of Salisbury City Hall. Shortly after UDI it was not unusual to see motor vehicles loaded with barrels of petrol arriving in front of the City Hall. They bore placards stating that these gifts of petrol were a gesture of support from South African colleagues. A lone cyclist, who had cycled all the way from the Transvaal with a small can of petrol, also arrived to give practical and psychological aid to his white compatriots in Rhodesia.

It is noteworthy that the majority of ministers (and also parliamentarians) in the Rhodesian Front government were either British-born or the descendants of British immigrants. A number of Cabinet ministers flaunted British army ranks and the Cabinet even included a noble lord. There were surprisingly large numbers of renegade Englishmen in the population at large. If asked, they were quick to say why they had immigrated to Rhodesia. The usual story was that they were unable to contend with the frustrations and discomfort of living in England as a welfare state that stifled initiative, and that England had become too liberal and allowed too many coloured immigrants to enter the country. They admitted that living in Rhodesia with its glorious climate, cheap servants and cheap labour was very desirable. Despite their ready condemnation of the old country, the land of their birth, they all chose to retain their British nationality and would troop down to South Africa to renew their passports in Pretoria when the British High Commission in Rhodesia was closed following UDI.

At a tennis party one afternoon a Rhodesian Army medical officer was pleased to relate the story of how he had recently returned from Pretoria where he had obtained a new British passport. When he arrived back home his family and friends did a war dance around him and spat on the passport, which was placed on the floor. This unpleasant story was typical of the attitude of a British renegade at that time. They all sported a sticker on the back of their cars which bluntly stated 'I HATE HAROLD'. This referred to Harold Wilson, the British prime minister. The majority of European driven cars in Salisbury had the same message stuck on their rear ends! We have always contended that if the British government had had the tenacity to refuse to issue passports to British subjects who actively supported the mutinous regime in Rhodesia, the rebellion may have come to a premature end!

The British South Africa Police had changed out of all recognition from the force I had known and worked with in Bulawayo in 1939 and again at Victoria Falls. Recruits no longer came from the middle or upper-middle classes in Britain, where they enlisted to seek a life of adventure in remote parts of the Empire. There was little change in the African members of the force, but the recent expansion in police personnel, needed to cope with the increasing crime and disorder, had resulted in the recruitment of young Rhodesian and South African lads into the force.

It was about this time that its reputation began to change. No longer was it the fine, decent, disciplined, gentlemanly body of men who maintained law and order through cooperation with the races rather than through the use of force. Individual European members of the force were now often curt and rude when dealing with the public and it was alleged that the police frequently used violence and were even accused of brutality in dealing with African suspects or miscreants. They were no longer the friends, but had become the enemies, of the African population. In the course of my work I met a couple of senior members of the BSAP who admitted they were very unhappy with the turn of events and were counting the days until they were able to retire and return to England. At the time when General Anderson was retired from his post as officer in command of military forces, the commissioner of police publicly stated his support for the RF government.

The only organized opposition to the oppressive extreme right-wing government came from the Christian churches and from staff and students at the University of Rhodesia and Nyasaland in Salisbury. The Christian churches had a united front against the Smith government and continued to carry on with their non-racial ministry, disregarding the Land Apportionment Act which guaranteed racial separation or apartheid in the country. South Africa had its Father Huddleston; Rhodesia had Bishop Kenneth Skelton, who was the Church of England's bishop of Matabeleland in Bulawayo, and Bishop Lamont of the Catholic Church in Umtali who both openly confronted the government and criticized its unchristian attitude. Meanwhile, official propaganda proclaimed this same hypocritical government as the defender of the Christian way of life in Africa and beyond! It is to the credit of the Christian churches that they refused to sanctify or give approval to the UDI. It was reported that Smith had to obtain his spiritual support and blessing from a Bulawayo rabbi. Because of their non-racial ministrations and refusal to support UDI, the Christian churches were the most effective opposition to what Bishop Lamont and his German nuns described as a government reminiscent of the Nazi government in Germany. The church leaders declined to attend official functions and refuted Smith's claim that his government was responsible for maintaining 'Christian standards' in the country. My sons, who were at boarding school near Bulawayo, described how Bishop Skelton had argued with and tried to convert some of the boys who supported the Rhodesian Front to become reasonable young men. Unfortunately he had little success. It was reported from overseas that the Archbishop of Canterbury had advised Prime Minister Wilson that the use of force to put down the Rhodesian insurrection would have the support of the Church of England, much to the annoyance of the Rhodesian Front supporters.

As I mention earlier, the University of Rhodesia and Nyasaland was like an oasis in a desert of racial prejudice. All races mixed freely and were on intimate terms within the confines of the campus. There were, however, a couple of dives on the edge of the city centre where left-wing European students met and mixed with black friends. A few lecturers became involved in African politics and a historian by the name of Terence Ranger joined an African nationalist party and was openly aggressive towards the Smith government until such time as he was deported. A lecturer was imprisoned after being found guilty of smuggling arms and explosives to the nationalists. Because my eldest son was a student at the university, which was becoming the last refuge of sanity in the country, we often came into contact with professors, lecturers and liberal students. Practically all the university staff were expatriates and, while most of them condemned the activities of the Smith government, only a few took an active part in politics. Following UDI they sent letters to the press, locally and overseas, condemning and refusing to accept the legality of the government. Some of the liberal students, especially the girls, became psychologically affected by events following the declaration; they were regular visitors to our home. The way lecturers and students were disparaged and physically attacked at political meetings has already been described. A number of students and staff were ardent Rhodesian Front supporters who also acted as police informers. My son was among a small number of university staff and students invited to attend the festivities in Lusaka to celebrate the granting of independence to Northern Rhodesia under President Kaunda.

Eventually most of the professors and lecturers either left the country or did not renew their contracts. Others were deported. The principal of the university, Dr Adams, was opposed to government policy and threatened to resign because of harassment of black students by the police, but eventually served out his term of engagement. He was criticized by many of his students and colleagues for his compromising attitude to the government when they had been so hostile to the university, which was subsequently placed under police supervision. This interference in a learning institution naturally led to a lowering of its academic standards and loss of prestige in world academic circles.

Nearly all the university staff who left the territory returned to the United Kingdom, where they were highly regarded in their various disciplines and, as a rule, had little difficulty obtaining senior posts in British universities. We contacted some of them later when visiting the UK. The senior classics lecturer was given an appointment at a Cambridge University college, the lecturer in politics a post at the University of York, and another became a professor at the Open University. A couple of the medical staff became leaders in their profession in England and Dr Adams was appointed director of the London School of Economics.

The university staff were not the only people leaving Rhodesia; emigration increased before and immediately after UDI. The emigrants would most likely have been from the more enlightened section of the European community. They were replaced to a certain extent by new immigrants (many of whom came from newly-independent African territories in the north) and by right-wing enthusiasts and mercenaries who obviously found the Smith regime acceptable. With the exception of South Africa and Portugal, most of the foreign embassies closed after UDI and Salisbury began to lose its cosmopolitan atmosphere.

As time passed my employment with the city council continued to be unaffected, but the constant barrage of right-wing political propaganda and the absence of reliable news made the politically-conscious among us feel demoralized. An increasing number of people were being held without trial or were being deported, including the chairman of the Guild of Journalists, who for some reason was considered subversive and was deported without warning. I intuitively felt we should emigrate, regardless of the consequences, especially because of the future of our two sons. My wife, who did not come into daily contact with colleagues (who by now were mostly keen Rhodesian Front supporters), was reluctant to emigrate until we knew exactly where we would be going; and it was understandable that she did not wish to abandon our lovely home and garden and leave her many good friends. It was providence that guided our predestination in two respects.

My eldest son, who had recently graduated from the University of Rhodesia and Nyasaland with a University of London degree in economics was granted a Commonwealth scholarship to Cambridge University to read for a PhD in economics. It was with a feeling of both sadness and satisfaction that we saw him off on the morning mail train to Beira, from where he sailed up the east coast of Africa, through the Suez Canal and the Mediterranean Sea to England. We were sad because we would miss him, but pleased, not only because of the opportunity he had been given to further his studies at Cambridge University, but also (and even more so) because we were concerned that he would be restricted or even incarcerated for his overt activities against our oppressive government.

A short while later I received a phone call from the medical officer of health in Lusaka. He informed me that he had decided to resign from his appointment at the end of the year, for personal reasons, and suggested I apply for the post. I accepted his suggestion with alacrity and in due course flew to Lusaka for an interview with the Lusaka City Council Health Committee. There were two other candidates for the post, who were both well-qualified ex-colonial medical officers. I was fortunate to be chosen for the position. It was now nearing the end of 1966 and during the next couple of months we were busy selling our house and arranging for our departure.

I asked my friend Malcolm Smith, editor of the local daily newspaper, the *Rhodesia Herald*, not to mention my new appointment in the press, as it would lead to condemnation by councillors and others if they knew I had resigned and was leaving to be employed by a non-European council in an adjacent territory. As an illustration of how events had degenerated in Rhodesia, I received a phone call from one of Malcolm Smith's underlings at the *Rhodesia Herald* news office who rudely informed me that my request to his editor would be ignored and my appointment as MOH in Lusaka would be published, which it was on the front page the next day. As anticipated, councillors and colleagues showed their displeasure. At the last committee meeting I attended a woman councillor said, 'You should be ashamed of yourself because you are absconding and betraying your fellow Europeans in Central Africa.'

We managed to sell our house in the last week of December. My wife, younger son and two dogs set off for Lusaka in our two cars on the last day of the year. We arrived there, after an uneventful journey, later the same day. I was surprised to see that the customs officer on the Zambia side of the border at Chirundu Bridge was a young European whom I had treated for polio in Livingstone ten years previously.

6

Zambia: Lusaka

D uring the drive from Salisbury to Lusaka it was inevitable
that we would reflect on the reason why we felt we had to
leave Rhodesia. The main thought that entered my mind
was the unexpected inaction of the government in the United
Kingdom. Rhodesia was a colony and Britain had a responsibility
to deal with the insurrection. If only rebels had been refused
British passports, or if minimum force such as the occupation of
Salisbury airport had been sanctioned, we may have remained in
our pleasant environment in Salisbury. I recollected the day when
Sir Alec Douglas-Home, as Her Majesty's colonial secretary, had
informed me personally in Livingstone more than ten years
previously that the projected Central African Federation had an
enviable economic future. If only politicians realized that 'man
doth not live on bread alone', or if only the Rhodesian African
nationalists had not boycotted the 1962 and subsequent general
elections and used their A and B roll voting strength, the
Rhodesian Front would not have won the election and circumstances may well have turned out differently.

On arrival in Lusaka we were gratified that we had been
allocated a recently completed, adequate house in a pleasant part
of the city near the president's residence and opposite the golf
course. It had three bedrooms, two bathrooms, a front veranda
and a large underdeveloped garden, which was unfenced. We soon
learned that it was the policy of the local authority not to fence
private properties in order to encourage neighbourliness. I mention
this because, a couple of weeks after our arrival, all our veranda

furniture (tables and chairs) was stolen during the night. I hastily planted a quick growing boundary hedge.

On our first night in Lusaka we attended a party, previously arranged, at the house of an old friend who was the principal of the government law school in the city. The party was held to celebrate New Year's Eve, our arrival in Zambia and the departure of three of our host's friends, officials at the British High Commission, who were being transferred to a posting outside Zambia. In the early hours of the morning, when we were all very merry, our acquaintances from the High Commission lost some of their earlier reserve. When I questioned them about the reason for their group transfer, they answered that 'Britain was giving up the nursery stakes' and was about to become part of Europe. In this thought-provoking reply it was obvious that by 'nursery stakes' they meant developing ex-colonial territories, and that the decision to join the European Common Market had been taken long before the referendum in the UK. The eventual entry of the United Kingdom into the market six years later, in 1972, showed that important political decisions are not as fortuitous as is commonly perceived.

When I reached my office in the Lusaka City Hall the next day, the first working day of my new appointment, I was surprised to be greeted by a press reporter and photographer. A photograph and article on the front page of the next morning's *Zambia Mail* announced my arrival. I was astounded by the size and splendour of my air-conditioned office, luxuriously furnished with a large executive desk and also a large table and chairs for staff meetings. Enormous containers with ferns and flowers were tastefully displayed alongside the walls. A door at one end of the room led to my private secretary's office and another to that of the chief health inspector. There was ample accommodation for clerical and other staff. I was met by the town clerk and introduced to the other chief council officers, who, with the exception of the housing officer, were all expatriate Europeans, as were their deputies and senior staff. For the first time I experienced the sensation of feeling important; but this was only ephemeral when I discovered that my professional employment entailed a far larger range of endeavour that I had anticipated. My full title would be MEDICAL OFFICER OF

HEALTH AND WELFARE IN CHARGE OF THE DEPARTMENT OF HEALTH AND WELFARE. It was the welfare title which bothered me because I had no practical experience in the administration of social services. There was no need to be apprehensive because I was lucky to have a university professor and senior lecturer in sociology (both Americans) attached to the welfare section of the department. Their help in overcoming difficulties that arose was inestimable.

I soon settled into my routine responsibilities. At the outset I realized that the council was organized and administered in much the same way as it had been in Salisbury. The Health Committee and council meetings I had to attend produced the same uninformative minutes. There was little difference between black and white politicians, with the proviso that black politicians were less sophisticated in their deliberations. Their previous white mentors had done their job well in enlightening them about restricted polemic. There was only one white councillor, a German refugee resident who did not seem to fit in at all. It was not long before he was replaced by a Zambian and thereafter I had to work with an all black council.

There was an adequate environmental health division in the department. It employed ten British-trained health inspectors and a large cleaning and refuse removal service (over 400 African labourers under a European superintendent), as well as food inspection and pest control sections, also under European supervision. My private secretary was a European woman. Zambia had been given its independence under a black government in October 1964 and I had expected the Africanization of government and local authority officials and staff to have gone further than it had during the two years since then. However, this was to be changed in the near future. The director of medical services of the whole country was a very pleasant young Zambian doctor who was always willing to discuss his problems with experienced senior medical colleagues.

Following the granting of independence in African territories it was the tendency for inhabitants living in rural areas to move to the large conurbations where they expected to find it easier to obtain employment and to live more fulfilling and exciting lives. Zambia was no exception to this rule and Lusaka was reputed to be the most rapidly growing city in the world! New residents poured into the city by their thousands and those who were unable to obtain suitable housing or accommodation with relatives settled in squatter suburbs on the outskirts of the city. These unofficial outlying suburbs consisted of primitive self-erected hovels made of odd pieces of corrugated iron, plywood or even cardboard. There was no piped pure water supply and no sewage disposal. Numerous wells for their water and pit latrines were dug in close proximity to each other. These unofficial squatter suburbs presented us with a potential health hazard because of the unhygienic environment in which the residents lived. As predicted, it was not long before waterborne infectious diseases, such as typhoid and dysentery, began to be notified. It became essential to trace the source of the infection and, to do so, one had to assume the attributes of a detective. I had a rough map made of the affected suburb and a pin with a red flag was stuck into each hovel from which a case was reported. The probable source of the outbreak became evident by observing the distribution of the red flags. The water in the adjacent well would then be sent for bacteriological examination and, if positive, the well would immediately be filled in by the engineers' department and new cases would cease to be reported. To control an outbreak of typhoid or dysentery successfully gave one deep personal satisfaction. It was a procedure that most public-health workers would desire to accomplish, but which few were ever given the opportunity to achieve.

Zambia was a country that depended on a mono-economy. Most of its revenue came from copper and, as this was a period when the price of the metal was high, general prosperity in the country and in Lusaka was evident. The government and local authority wisely provided funds for the provision of high-density housing in the city and as many as 16 houses to the acre were rapidly constructed with pure-water standpipes and waterborne sewage. Plots were also made available for residents to erect their own homes with cheap building materials sold to them by the council. Help in construction was given by VSO personnel. This resulted in a commendable operation to help overcome the housing shortage in a relatively short time.

Although the environmental and welfare divisions of the department were well developed and adequate, personal health provision was virtually non-existent. I lost no time in inaugurating this essential service. Health visitors and a clinic nurse were appointed, and child welfare, immunization, nutrition and antenatal clinics began to be held regularly in the city suburbs. A new large public-health clinic was established in the central city council building. Eventually six well-qualified health visitors were appointed, of which only one was a European. We did not undertake any curative medicine; this was left entirely to the government health services. The relatively small number of European residents did not need to take advantage of the personal public-health services provided and our efforts were mainly directed to the more needy residents, especially those in the new squatter suburbs. The provision of health education was also upgraded.

With the steady increase of the population and the extension of the city boundaries, the work and staff of the welfare division was expanded to a commensurate degree. Under the influence of our American advisers the title of the division was changed from 'welfare' to that of 'community development' because the name welfare suggested the provision of largesse to those requiring help and this branch of the social services was the responsibility of the government welfare department. The concept of community development meant that residents in all townships were encouraged to help their neighbours who were in need. We provided suburban halls where stage shows, dances and other indoor entertainments could be arranged. Sports facilities and indoor and outdoor cinema shows were also provided in each suburb. Community development was a vast improvement on the previous practice of welfare. Residents in each suburb, under the guidance of the community development officer, held dances, concerts, sports meetings and other social entertainment in order to raise cash to help those needing help in their own areas. The council contributed pound for pound (*kwatcha* for *kwatcha*) for money collected by residents on their own initiative or enterprise.

Trained social workers continued to deal with the individual cases requiring help in hospitals or in their own homes, and they also supervised the provision of adult literacy classes. The ramifications of public-health needs, provided by the environmental division of the department, created a vast undertaking. It included the provision of public cleansing as well as refuse removal and disposal, meat and food inspection, the control of infectious diseases and pest control. The Public Health Acts in Zambia had been copied from the English acts, with one important additional proviso. This was that 'no food or drink for human consumption was to be prepared, packed, conveyed or sold without an annual licence issued by the Medical Officer of Health.' This made it comparatively easy to supervise and ensure the hygienic preparation and sale of food and drink. If any person or organization was found to be unhygienic in their handling of food or drink for human consumption, their licence to operate was cancelled or refused.

Pest control included the eradication of rats, which could spread plague and other diseases, and also the control of dogs, especially in the advent of an outbreak of rabies, when all stray dogs were caught and put into our dog pound or shot if behaving in a strange manner. The brain was sent to the veterinary department to ascertain if it was infected with rabies. In my experience the report invariably came back positive because it involved too much responsibility on the part of the veterinarians to submit a negative report. All individuals who were bitten by (or came into contact with the saliva of) the rabid animal had to undergo a course of prophylactic anti-rabies virus inoculations, which were given under the skin of the abdomen and were painful. The injections were given daily for 14 days at the end of which time the patients and the doctor administering the vaccine were fed up with each other! At the present time the diagnosis of rabies in the suspected animal and the administration of anti-rabies vaccine directly into the muscle has made it easier for all concerned.

Following the routine examination of urine specimens from all the children at a Lusaka primary school, over 50 per cent were found to show the presence of the eggs of the schistosome worm, which lived in the veins of the bladder and caused the disease known as bilharzia. This often resulted in the passing of blood in the urine and, if left untreated, could eventually lead to anaemia or other complications. Fresh-water snails are the intermediate hosts of the disease and humans were infected by swimming or wading in infected pools or streams when the worm (in its cercaria stage) would penetrate the skin. Prevention of the disease entailed providing a pure water supply and preventing the contamination of pools and streams with infected urine, which, in turn, required an adequate sewage disposal system. We introduced chemicals to kill all the snails in infected pools and the public, especially children, were advised not to swim or wade in adulterated streams. There was a notable decrease in the incidence of the disease.

Malaria was endemic throughout Zambia and was more prevalent in hot, damp areas such as the Zambezi Valley. Infection occurs as the result of a bite by a female anopheles mosquito, which, in turn, has been infected by biting an individual infected with the malaria parasite in his or her blood, and so the cycle continues. It is important that all cases of malaria are diagnosed, by finding a positive blood smear, and treated in order to help prevent the spread of the infection. Untreated cases can develop complications and even die. The symptoms of malarial infection are more acute, with severe headache and high temperature, in Europeans than in the indigenous population, where the symptoms are less pronounced. This indicates some immunity to the disease, but no malarial antibodies have ever found in the blood and an antimalarial vaccine has not been produced to date.

The prevention of malaria, in addition to the treatment of all active cases, consists of taking prophylactic antimalarial drugs by residents and visitors in an area where malaria is known to be prevalent. It is of interest to record that when I first came to Rhodesia, tablets of quinine were issued free at all post offices for use as a daily antimalarial prophylactic drug. In my experience, the irregular taker of quinine could develop a serious complication of malaria known as blackwater fever, which was a condition in which the unfortunate patient's red blood corpuscles broke down and the resulting debris blocked the kidney tubules. It was usually fatal. With the introduction of chemotherapeutic prophylactic drugs to replace the use of quinine, the dreaded condition of blackwater fever became a thing of the past.

To prevent mosquito bites it was advisable to sleep under mosquito nets and cover bare parts of the body after dark, which

151

was when the female mosquito developed a hunger for a meal of human blood. Insecticides, in the form of an aerosol spray in the air, or a local application to the exposed parts of the skin, were useful mosquito repellents. With the discovery of DDT, a powerful insecticide, in the early 1940s, the walls of all railway houses and premises in malarial areas in Southern and Northern Rhodesia were sprayed with it. This left the walls looking untidy, with a powdery covering, but it was no longer necessary to sleep under a mosquito net. Employees who refused to have their houses sprayed were warned that they would lose sick pay if they were off duty due to an attack of malaria. The procedure resulted in a significant fall in the number of cases of malaria, but DDT was later found to be toxic and its use was discontinued.

The only really effective method of controlling malaria is to prevent the breeding of the specific type of anopheles mosquito, which carries the malaria parasite, in the area to be controlled. In all the areas in which I worked in Zambia, only two types of mosquito were malaria parasite carriers. One of these was *Anopheles Gambia*. They bred in small pools of warm water, preferably muddy ones. Favourite sites were the holes left in soft soil by the hooves of domestic animals, or empty tins or other containers left around collecting rainwater, which was then warmed by the sun. It was easy to discern the mosquito larvae in these and other similar breeding sites. The other type of carrier was *Anopheles Fumestus*, which bred in slow-running shady streams. At Victoria Falls the banks of the Zambezi River were a favourite breeding place and the removal of foliage along the river bank was effective in eradicating the breeding of this particular insect vector. The spraying of oil on all small collections of water eradicated *Anopheles Gambia* and the area of the Victoria Falls Hotel became malaria free. It has since come to my notice that in recent years it is not unusual for staff and visitors to the Victoria Falls Hotel to become the victims of malarial infection.

Our pest control section in Lusaka included a foreman and a gang of sprayers expressly employed to carry out the spraying of suspected breeding sites of *Anopheles Gambia*. Malaria was a notifiable disease in the city and every case reported was fully investigated by our staff. To cover the incubating period of the disease it would be necessary to find out where the patient had been ten to 14 nights before the onset of fever. Over a period of years we were not able to trace even one case of a patient being infected in the city area, so it became unnecessary for Lusaka residents or visitors to take any antimalarial precautions. The fact that all reported cases of malaria in the city were contracted outside the city area gave me and my staff a sense of satisfaction.

The World Health Organization was actively engaged in a campaign to reduce the incidence of smallpox worldwide and we were frequently visited by a Russian doctor in its employ who encouraged us to increase the number of residents being vaccinated against the disease. We acceded to his request by employing and training five full-time public vaccinators to carry out the work. They commenced a house to house campaign and even approached residents walking in the streets or congregating in markets. It was surprising how cooperative the public were in accepting the inconvenience of being vaccinated. It was not long after this that the one and only case of smallpox was reported in Lusaka during my stay there. A medical practitioner in the city phoned to inform me that a member of the staff residing in the embassy of an adjacent African country had brought his young child to his surgery with a rash, which he had diagnosed as a definite case of smallpox. When informed of the diagnosis, the father refused to have the child isolated in hospital and took it back to the embassy. After due consideration I decided not to approach the foreign embassy, but instead to advise the appropriate government department about the position, with the request that they appeal to the embassy concerned, in the interest of public health, to allow the child to be admitted to the isolation hospital. I was given to understand that, after some difficulty and persuasion, the child was eventually sent to hospital where the diagnosis was confirmed. A pleasing aspect about this incident was that no further case of smallpox was reported, which showed that our vaccination campaign had been effective. A few years later smallpox was completely eradicated throughout the world.

The study and control of diseases peculiar to the tropics requires a knowledge of microscopy, zoology and entomology. It is a study of life itself. Taking malaria as an example, it is necessary to consider not only the disease in man, but its cycle in the mosquito. This requires an intimate knowledge of the life cycle and habits of the insect, as well as of the malaria parasite that causes the disease. There are many examples of one form of life invading another in order to sustain and propagate its own and human beings are sometimes the victims of their evolution. Bilharzia, which has already been considered, is a disease in which man is the definite host of the schistosome worm, which causes the complaint. Extensive knowledge of the life cycle of the worm and its intermediate host, which is a specific type of tropical snail, is needed to prevent the disease. Plague is the result of infection with a special type of bacteria which requires rats, fleas and man to complete its life cycle. Sleeping sickness, which is caused by a trypanosome parasite, requires cattle or game, the tsetse fly and human beings to complete its cycle. In smallpox, human beings themselves are the reservoir of the infectious organism (a virus, the smallest and most primitive form of zoological life to infect man) that causes the disease. Yellow fever is also caused by a virus carried from man to man by a mosquito named *Aedes Egypti*; it does not spread malaria. The discovery of the chemistry of genes in recent years has made scientists aware of the similarity of all forms of life. For example, pigs into which human genes have been transplanted excrete proteins similar to those of the human being!

* * *

When we arrived in Zambia, the country was still being adversely troubled by the unlawful UDI — the sanctions imposed on Rhodesia were affecting Zambia more than the country for which they were intended to apply. Zambia depended on Rhodesia and South Africa for manufactured goods, and on their ports for importing goods from abroad and exporting copper. When relations between Zambia and Rhodesia were broken off following UDI, copper could no longer be transported along the railway passing through Rhodesia, and oil and petrol could no longer be sent to Zambia from the refinery at the end of the Lonrho oil pipeline near Beira. As a stopgap, drums of oil and petrol were flown in by air from Dar es Salaam in Tanzania. From our house we were able to observe numerous plane loads of these drums arriving at the aerodrome all day long. It was paradoxical that petrol rationing was more severe in Zambia than in Rhodesia. As an emergency measure, copper was dispatched by road to Malawi and then by rail to Beira; the Benguela railways increased its capacity to carry extra copper for export through Angola. A road was hurriedly constructed for the 'hell run' between Zambia and Dar es Salaam for the importation of goods and the export of copper by motor transport.

President Kaunda and his advisers had been certain that the United Kingdom would use force to end the Rhodesian rebellion. They had therefore offered Zambia as a base from which military action could be taken. Prime Minister Wilson's refusal to use force placed Kaunda in an unenviable position, for it left Zambia open to attack from Rhodesia, which had taken over all the aircraft and most of the military equipment following the break-up of the federation. They also feared that South Africa might take advantage of the situation and also attack Zambia. Not long after our arrival in Lusaka, a medical colleague who had been on a fishing trip up the Zambezi River told me that he had seen South African troops along the south bank of the river where the Caprivi Strip (in South West Africa, then under South African mandate) borders the Zambezi. To forestall such an attack, the United Kingdom stationed a squadron of Javelin fighter aircraft at Lusaka airport, which were guarded by a company from the Royal Air Force regiment. This gave us a sense of personal security.

It did not take us long to settle down in Lusaka, especially since a number of our old friends from Broken Hill and Livingstone were now working and living in the city. Lusaka had become a modern metropolis with good facilities. It had adequate sports and social clubs, first-rate hotels and an up-to-date cinema. Its television service was worth viewing at times, but there was no live theatre. Entertaining in private houses was popular, but we soon noticed that, apart from the numerous official functions, there was no social mixing of the races in people's own homes.

Because of the extreme right-wing nature of the South African and Rhodesian governments, Russia, East Germany, Yugoslavia and numerous other European, eastern and African states did not place their diplomatic representatives in those countries. In any case I imagine they would have been considered *personae non gratae* there. As a result, Zambia's capital city became a convenient observation and listening post for all the countries without embassies in Rhodesia or South Africa. Because of the numerous legations — the council had allocated an avenue in the most desirable part of the city for the exclusive construction of foreign legations or embassies — a large proportion of the non-indigenous residents in the city were diplomats and their senior embassy personnel. This gave Lusaka a most agreeable international flavour. As a senior official in the city council, I was (along with the mayor, town clerk and other chief officers) automatically invited to the parties or banquets a number of countries held at their embassies to celebrate their various national days. These included the Queen's Birthday at the British Embassy, Independence Day at the US Embassy, Bastille Day at the French Embassy and Revolution Day at a large hall specially rented for the occasion by the Russians. These were usually lavish affairs with lashings of smoked salmon at the British Embassy, and bowls of black, red and yellow caviar at the Russian celebration. National drinks such as whisky or vodka were always freely available.

The fare provided at banquets, especially the ones the council held at a hotel, usually consisted of smoked Scotch salmon as a starter, cold fried chicken and salad as the main course, and a sweet. The smoked salmon was not acceptable to the Africans and we were not keen on the chicken, which was usually tough, so we came to an arrangement whereby we changed our chicken for their smoked salmon — a form of barter appreciated by all concerned!

We were never invited to the Chinese Embassy and the relationship between them and ourselves is worth recording. I received a deputation of two representatives from the refuse collection labourers in my department who had an extraordinary request; they wanted me to give them and their colleagues permission to attend a function at the Chinese Embassy. They seemed sceptical when I informed them that, unless they broke the law, what they did when they were not at work was no business of mine or the council's.

Our public-health clinic was open on three afternoons each week for the inoculation and vaccination of travellers who were issued with an international health book, which was demanded from them on arrival by most countries throughout the world. To conform with international public-health regulations, I had to sign each book that was issued. The average attendance was about ten persons at each clinic, but one sunny afternoon a large omnibus with 40 Chinamen aboard arrived at the clinic and requested to be inoculated against yellow fever and vaccinated against smallpox. When they descended from the bus and lined up outside the clinic, I saw a sight I shall never forget. They were all dressed alike in a pyjama-type suit, were the same height, had the same expression on their faces and appeared to be alike in every detail, like peas in a pod. It was difficult to estimate their ages, but I thought they were all in their early twenties. The gentleman in charge, who spoke English, was conspicuous by his different appearance. He was taller and thinner than his identical charges. As those were the days before the introduction of disposable plastic syringes, it was not possible for us to attend to this crowd in one afternoon; there were only ten syringes available and it took 20 minutes to sterilize them. Their leader seemed annoyed when I told him we would attend to ten members of his retinue today and that the others would have to attend an appointment on another day. When I asked him what this crowd of lookalikes were doing in Lusaka, his only reply was 'Doctor! You are an imperialist!' and departed with his flock. This was not the end of the matter. About an hour later I received a phone call from an irate Chinese ambassador who informed me that we ran an inadequate health service and that I was responsible for his being inconvenienced. My reply was no less brusque than his unjustified accusation.

While on the subject of Chinese influence in Zambia, I recall that for many years, even when we were stationed in Broken Hill, the construction of a railway between Broken Hill and Dar es Salaam, the most accessible port on the Indian Ocean, was considered, especially with regard to the benefits it would bring to Northern Rhodesia, making it so much easier and quicker for the export of copper and the importation of goods from abroad. When Zambia was established as an independent state in 1964, President Kaunda, conscious of the dependency of Zambia on Rhodesia and South Africa for rail transport, began to enquire into the feasibility of building such a railway line. Several organizations, including Lonrho, carried out surveys, but the cost was prohibitive and it was anticipated that there would be insufficient traffic to justify its construction. The Chinese who, unlike the Russians, were active in the propagation of communism in several African countries, offered to pay for and build the line. Kaunda was not keen on the offer because he suspected ulterior political motives, but under the influence of Nyerere, the president of Tanzania, through whose territory part of the line would pass, he agreed to its construction by the Chinese government and work on building the line commenced in 1970. In general, despite South African and Rhodesian opinions to the contrary, Africans were not amenable to conversion to communism and the vast amount of money and effort spent by the Chinese in Africa at that time was wasted.

I have described how fortunate we were to have had the opportunity to meet so many distinguished visitors at Victoria Falls, but Lusaka turned out to be even more favourable in this respect. It appeared to be the unofficial meeting place of the Organization of Unaligned Countries, and for one of its important meetings the Zambian government went to considerable lengths and expense to accommodate the delegates. It built special houses in the city centre and each mission was allocated one of these for their short stay in Lusaka. A large hall was also made available for their use with expensive furniture and fittings, and with special electrical installations for the complicated interpretation facilities. Cholera epidemics had been reported in several of the delegates' home countries and I was worried about the possibility of there being a carrier among those attending the meetings. Unknown to them, we took a specimen each day from the sewers leading away from the residences and halls they frequented. Fortunately we did not obtain a positive *Cholera vibrio* specimen.

There were frequent visits by heads of states who were invariably given a civic welcome, often followed by a reception in the beautiful gardens at State House, the president's residence, in the evenings. We were invited to all these numerous functions and, though they were interesting and enjoyable, one could have too much of a good thing! We wanted to lead our own private social life of visiting and entertaining personal friends, but hardly a week passed without an invitation to an embassy or official reception. We skipped a couple of these official functions thinking that our absence would go unnoticed in the large crowd. Unfortunately I was mistaken, for the only official rebuke I received during my period of employment in Lusaka was to the effect that my absence at certain official functions had been noted and that the mayor considered that, as a senior council official, it was part of my duties to help entertain distinguished foreign guests to the city. I have often cogitated about the significance of this matter and have come to the conclusion that it was a form of racism in reverse, a desire to show the world outside that Europeans were still happily employed and living in an independent black state.

We met dignitaries such as Mrs Gandhi, as well as President Tito and his wife, Mrs Brodz, who visited Zambia on a number of occasions. They were both very unassuming, but I have one complaint against Tito. We were able to buy very high-quality South African fruit, which was brought into the city each week in a refrigerated truck. We took advantage of this facility and would purchase various types of fruit by the case. This desirable amenity suddenly came to an end. The fruiterer was unable to explain why the supply had stopped, but the explanation was eventually leaked to us. Apparently President Tito had been staying with Dr Kaunda at State House and on one occasion remarked on the fine quality of the fruit being served. He said he would like to have it exported to Yugoslavia in large quantities. Kaunda had to admit that the fruit was imported from South Africa and Tito was so furious that an immediate ban was placed on its importation. Thereafter we were only able to purchase indifferent airlifted Greek and Italian fruit at exorbitant prices.

We also met the heads of African states. In addition to the usual evening receptions in the city hall or at a leading hotel, they would be entertained at informal morning or afternoon tea parties given by the mayor in his parlour. At these tea parties we were able to meet the dignitaries on a more intimate basis. I recall being very impressed by President Stevens of Sierra Leone, a tall erudite gentleman, but uninspired by President Mobutu of Zaire, who was surly, self-opinionated and did not remove his fur hat. These gatherings gave me the chance to meet and even sit next to our own president, so after a while I began to know him quite well.

President Kaunda was not photogenic. Like Prime Minister Attlee in England, his image on television was very different from his appearance in the flesh. He had a pleasant, handsome countenance, with a captivating smile. He had been educated at a mission school and was a schoolmaster before taking an interest in politics. He was one of the founders of (and became leader of) the United National Independence Party and, like most African nationalist leaders, was imprisoned twice before becoming head of state in 1964. He was a devout Christian with high moral principles. He was a confidante and friend of the Reverend Colin Morris, the head of the Methodist Church in Zambia, who eventually became head of the BBC's religious programmes. Kaunda was an emotional man; he always carried a clean handkerchief in his hand and would weep in public, even after only slight provocation.

As a democrat, he was against tribalism, did not advocate a one-party state and was disconcerted by the military coups in many recently-created independent states. He promoted what he considered to be the original philosophy of humanism. This exulted human beings, who were supposed to be at the centre of all endeavour. Should they fail to honour this dictum and be interested only in material gain, he felt, African progress would cease to be rewarding. He was not a racist and in his speeches always stressed the unimportance of a person's colour. His slogan, which he continually repeated, was 'ONE ZAMBIA, ONE NATION'. He became keen on golf and had a nine-hole course laid out in the grounds of State House. Like all beginners, his main topic of conversation, when not involved in the affairs of state, was golf. He had a fine deep voice and frequently sang African songs during receptions at State House.

I may have given the impression of being panegyrical in my portrayal of Dr Kaunda — he acquired his title from an honorary degree conferred on him by an American university — but he was the most pleasant and honest politician I have ever had the pleasure to meet. And leaders of the British Labour Party, Mr

Callaghan the prime minister in particular, were more complimentary about President Kaunda that I could ever be!

The president continued to have a difficult time coping with the
effects of the Rhodesian UDI. Stocks of copper began to accumu-
late at the copper mines because of the difficulties encountered in
exporting the metal. This led to the loss of millions of pounds from
taxation, while government expenditure was rising. The United
Kingdom refused to pay Zambia compensation for the loss and the
relationship between the two countries became strained. Smith
remained truculent in Rhodesia while the Wilson government
persisted in its refusal to use force; it sent out various notables to
Rhodesia to attempt to bring about a settlement. This was no more
successful than when Wilson himself later met Smith on the
battleship *Tiger* and subsequently on the *Fearless* in Gibraltar;
negotiations failed to bring about a result.

There were insufficient educated and trained Zambians available
to staff the civil service; the government and city council had to
depend on large numbers of expatriates on contracts to keep the
services efficient. European and African education had been
conducted separately in Northern Rhodesia under the colonial
administration and the most glowing example of the government's
incompetence was its failure to develop African education. We
remember the director of African education in Livingstone as a
very affable, likeable gentleman who took his duties lightly and
spent most of his time shooting spur-winged geese. The enrolment
of secondary school children had increased from 10,000 in 1964,
at the time of independence, to 35,000 in 1967.

When I first arrived back in the north, which was now Zambia
under black rule, I experienced a feeling of freedom after having
emigrated from the oppressive, fascist state of Rhodesia, but at the
same time I have to admit that I was concerned about the outlook
for race relations. I soon discovered that there had been no need to
feel apprehensive because, with few exceptions, now that they
were in power, Zambians did not seek retribution for the manner
in which they had been treated in the past. Because they were
complicated, I find it difficult to describe race relations as I
experienced them in Lusaka. Attitudes were characterized by
extreme points of view, and the following episode may help

elucidate my concerns about the subject. Most weekends my wife and I played tennis together at the Lusaka Club, but during the week she played there on her own with friends because I usually left my office too late to join them. However, I often stopped in at the club on my way home and joined them for a drink when they had finished playing. We were friendly with the Nigerian ambassador, a cultured gentleman, an Oxbridge graduate and a good tennis player with a fine physique. I arrived at the club one afternoon as usual and was sitting on a bench watching my wife partner him in a game of mixed doubles. A well-dressed, well-spoken Englishman, whom I had never met before, sat next to me on the bench and in the course of conversation casually remarked that the lady partnering the black chap should be ashamed of herself because she disregarded the standing of her own race. When I angrily pointed out that the lady in question was my wife, he quickly rose, apologized and walked away before I was able to tell him what was on my mind. In contrast to this sort of behaviour there were many Europeans, especially business people who had lived in Zambia before independence, who fell over backwards to gratify the Africans. I personally found this attitude discreditable. For the most part expatriates, like myself, came to the country to do a job of work and were not involved in politics. It did not matter to them that the Africans were now in command. We accepted the exasperation engendered by the inefficiency of Zambian employees and realized this was only to be expected. In general I would assume that the attitude of the majority of expatriates was disingenuous because they had a subconscious, deep-seated sense of superiority.

The few Zambians who could be described as anti-European were important because of the unpleasantness they created. The chief clerk in my department, who may or may not have been anti-European, was appointed from 'above' because he was alleged to have been a leading fighter during the so-called struggle for independence and this was his reward. He was an overbearing, unpleasant individual whose disruptive machinations were directed towards those who were in the more senior posts and happened to be Europeans. As a result of his unpleasantness my chief health inspector, a normally placid reasonable person, lost his cool and called him a monkey. As a result of this he was punched and knocked to the floor, but more seriously he had to leave the country in a hurry. The same sort of unpleasantness culminated in the rapid departure from Zambia of the American sociologist working in the community development division. I thought it inadvisable to meet the gentleman concerned head-on because I was aware of the influence he had in high places, and he was careful not to offend me in any way. There were one or two others like him working in the department and they made my position as head of the department similar to walking on a tightrope each day.

Another reason why living and working in Zambia was difficult was the high incidence of petty and more serious thieving. The disappearance of our veranda furniture shortly after our arrival has already been noted. This was followed by the theft of the radio from my car — it had been pulled out with a crowbar, which caused severe damage to the dashboard. The next year my car was stolen and recovered by the police in the bush near Broken Hill. The police told me that a gang of criminals stole cars in Zambia and drove them over the border into Zaire, where fences paid high prices for large stolen cars. These were driven from Lusaka to the border through the bush. This was because police patrols stopped cars on the main road and arrested anyone driving a car in which the ignition wires had been disconnected. The bumpy drive through the bush had not do my car much good; it had run out of petrol and its unusual presence there had been reported to the police.

One day my wife and I came home at lunch time and closed the front door behind us. My wife left her handbag containing cash, bank card and the usual contents carried in a bag belonging to a female on a table. When she later had reason to use the bag she was unable to find it. As the servants were unable to account for the missing bag, we reported the loss to the police, who informed us that we were the third household in our street who had suffered the same loss at lunch time on the same day. Needless to say it was never recovered.

A large amount of money was paid into my department by the public for various services carried out in the peri-urban area, such as the emptying of septic tanks. The clerks in the front office would issue receipts for the cash, which would then be handed over to the city treasurer's department at the end of each day. There were frequent complaints from the city treasurer that the cash paid into his department did not tally with the receipts. Furthermore, members of the public complained about receiving accounts rendered after they had paid their bills. It was later discovered that the receipt counterfoil in our office had been destroyed. This was a recurring source of annoyance to me and I eventually persuaded the city treasurer to take over all my department's cash transactions, but, believe it or not, this did not entirely end the dishonesty. When a member of the public came into our department to settle an account, instead of directing him or her to the treasurer's department, a member of my office staff would volunteer to take the money up to the treasurer's department on their behalf and, once again, there were discrepancies in the cash received. I had no alternative but to prohibit entirely the handling of public money by my staff.

A Lusaka resident was doing a major service on his car in his garage at home. He removed the back axle, which he placed outside the garage door, and went inside his house to have a cup of tea. When he came out his axle was missing. Neighbours told him that council refuse workers had been into his garden while he was indoors. He contacted us and, on making enquiries, the refuse workers concerned admitted that they had removed the axle; it had been lying next to the refuse bin and they had thought it was part of the refuse. We accepted their explanation, but when they admitted that they had sold the axle to a motor spare-parts dealer, they were charged with theft, reprimanded and fined. The axle was recovered and returned to its owner. Refuse was the property of the council and it was illegal for employees to sell any part of it for their own gain.

Though we found the Zambian police very courteous and helpful, its efficiency could hardly be described as exceptional. We were, however, dismayed by a report that a European criminal had managed to steal a firearm from the Lusaka central police station. The press reported that the president had carried out an unannounced inspection of all the police stations in Lusaka one night, but did not give details of his findings. An Australian health inspector in our department told me that he was friendly with the police and was a frequent visitor to their mess-bar in the central police station. On the night the president made his surprise inspection of the station he was in the bar and, together with a number of women, who should not have been there, managed to escape the attention of the president by climbing through a back window when he was inspecting the front of the building!

It was about this time that the refuse workers in my department appealed to the council for an increase in their rates of pay and I supported their claim, but when it was rejected by the appropriate council committee they went on strike. Because of the hot climate this created a public-health problem of the first magnitude. From the beginning the matter was completely taken out of my control by the government. President Kaunda was out of the country and the acting president, Simon Kapepwe, took charge of the disagreement and lived up to his reputation of being a tough citizen. At first convicts were brought in to collect the refuse, but when they began to throw it from their lorries at passing cars and pedestrians the scheme had to be abandoned. Large numbers of police arrived at the main refuse depot and the workers were ordered to return to work, which they refused to do. When armed troops arrived at the depot they decided to capitulate and resume their usual employment. A knowledge of industrial psychology was unnecessary for anyone employed to control a large labour force in a newly-independent African country such as Zambia.

An exceptionally bright young Zambian who had joined the police and was destined to become the commissioner was killed when his new Mercedes sports car crashed on the north road near Lusaka by hitting an obstruction. No other moving vehicle was involved in the crash. In this respect it is of interest to report that road accidents were the main cause of death in adults in Lusaka. Taking into account that few elderly Africans resided in the city, but stayed in their villages, road accidents accounted for nearly 50 per cent of all deaths. I asked the pathologist to have blood samples taken from the bodies of all road accident victims for chemical analysis. The results were startling. In some cases the alcohol content was so high that the victim would not have been able to have stood erect without support before death occurred.

It was the practice of many Lusaka European residents, including ourselves, to drive to Salisbury at long weekends, such as Easter, to meet old friends, attend a theatre or nightclub and take advantage of other amenities not available in Lusaka. Members of the British High Commission, among whom we had many friends, had been instructed not to visit Rhodesia because of UDI. Surprisingly, however, one of its female secretaries disregarded the instructions and openly visited Salisbury on every possible occasion. On one trip down, which used to take about four hours, we had to drive in convoy from some distance on the other side of the border because an armed terrorist, or what could be described as a freedom fighter, was at large in the bush adjoining the road. On our return three days later he was still at large.

After our arrival in Salisbury we were approached by various friends and acquaintances, also from Lusaka and staying at the same hotel, to lend them cash. They all had the same complaint. On an open straight road in an uninhabited part of the country near Sinoia, the first town encountered after entering Rhodesia, a small sign restricting the speed to 30 miles per hour had been put up and the BSAP had set up speed traps. All those caught exceeding the (unwarranted) speed limit were fined on the spot, depending on their speed, and were warned that those who did not pay their fine would be stopped on their way back and would have to appear in court in Sinoia on a day convenient to the magistrate. Hence the request for the loan of cash. Luckily we had left Lusaka later than the main crowd of travellers and so missed the speed trap. This was an example of how nasty the Rhodesian authorities could be to visitors from Zambia.

The primary reason for reporting this trip to Salisbury is to reflect on the extraordinary frame of mind of the members of a family we had known well when we had resided there. They were less friendly than usual, but enquired, in detail, how we were getting on in Lusaka. When we informed them that we were perfectly happy there and that their concern about our safety was unwarranted, the senior member of the family then informed us, in all seriousness, that Europeans were being confined in dungeons in the cellars below State House in Lusaka and that we had better be careful in future. I naturally refuted this ridiculous allegation and became so annoyed when they persisted in their story that I offered to pay the air fares for two of them to visit Lusaka and stay with us in order to find out the truth. The offer was not taken up!

Zambianization of the council staff was now being accomplished more actively. My European secretary was replaced by a South African Xhosa woman who, having spent the previous five years working as a private secretary in the City of London, knew all the answers. She returned to South Africa a short while later and, before leaving, had the temerity to tell me that she would use her influence to make me the MOH of Johannesburg in the next few years when there would be black rule in that unhappy country. She in turn was replaced by an Indian woman from Tanzania, who also proved to be an efficient secretary. We appointed our first non-European health inspector, who had qualified in the United Kingdom, and recruited six young Zambian trainee health inspectors for a three-year apprenticeship with us, after which they would obtain a Zambian health inspector's diploma. The town clerk, whom I found unhelpful, was illegally dismissed by the council and he also left the country in a hurry. He was replaced by a hopelessly inefficient Zambian.

When our American advisers returned to the United States, we advertised for a director of the community development section and were embarrassed by the hundreds of applications we received from all over the world, but mainly from the United States. I chose whom I considered to be the three most suitable candidates. The Establishment Committee persisted in delaying the appointment and it eventually became clear that it intended to appoint a suitable Zambian to the post when such a person became available. They blamed the delay on the Foreign Office, which objected to the post being filled by an overseas incumbent. When I recommended appointing the chief government health officer in Tanzania, who had applied to fill the vacancy of chief health officer in our department, the Establishment Committee turned down my recommendation because, as they baldly stated, he was an Englishman and we already had too many English expatriates working in the council! They then appointed a Greek Cypriot from Cyprus who, unbeknown to them, had qualified in and worked in England!

All these changes, along with the activities of dishonest councillors, were making it very difficult for chief officers to administer their departments properly. The head of the housing department, the only non-European chief officer, confided in me that certain councillors had compelled him to provide accommodation for their mistresses. Councillors were also involved in the Mafia-like cooperative that ran the city's markets, which incidentally caused us continual trouble and antagonism because of their lack of cleanliness. Rumours were circulating about the illegal granting of building plots to the mayor, who was a building contractor, and also to other councillors.

As was usual in this type of disreputable behaviour it was left to the president to clear up the mess and he appointed a commission of inquiry, consisting of three Europeans presided over by a judge, to enquire into the 'conduct of the affairs of the Lusaka City Council'. Their long report was damning, especially with regard to the illegal conduct of the acting town clerk, the mayor and certain other councillors. The irregular appointments of staff and the improper allocation of housing were also mentioned in the report. What became apparent to me was the undisguised naivety of the town clerk and councillors; this made them so different from the more sophisticated European councillors I had known in the past. A European senior government official was imposed on the council by the government to act as a temporary town clerk. He was eventually replaced by an efficient Basuto lawyer, a graduate of Trinity College, Dublin, who had been refused the right to practise as an advocate in a European-designated area in his native South Africa. From then on the conduct of the council administration and the behaviour of the councillors improved appreciably.

My employment continued to be interesting and rewarding, but at times I found it difficult to cope with the demands on my time. Over 20 outside depots or other centres of activity such as community halls, refuse disposal sites, clinics and many other work places had to be visited regularly, unannounced, in order to keep them up to scratch; it was not unusual to find employees absent without leave. I invariably had difficulty with the Establishment Committee when I wished to dismiss inefficient or incompetent staff. I did not consider I was being paranoiac when I thought that this was a case of councillors objecting to the dismissal of Zambians by a European expatriate! We were advised that the government intended to incorporate small peri-urban councils into Lusaka in the near future and this would create added responsibility and staff. My request to the Health Committee to appoint a deputy MOH was readily granted. On my next visit to the United Kingdom I interviewed an Indian doctor working as a deputy MOH in England and recommended his appointment as the most suitable candidate. He was well-qualified and experienced and soon settled down to his duties after his arrival in Lusaka. The salary we offered in Lusaka was higher than that paid for an equivalent post in the UK, so it was surprising that not one suitable European applied for the vacancy! At the same time my own three-year contract with the council was drawing to an end. I was asked to renew it for another three years, but, although we were very happy living in Lusaka, the prospect of another three years of balancing on a tightrope did not appeal to me. It was mutually agreed to extend my contract for one more year.

During my period of service as MOH I had some odd requests and visitors. Cabinet ministers and high-grade civil servants, including judges, lived in expensive, spacious, luxurious government houses with large gardens in a select part of the city. It was customary for Africans to have large extended families and to accept mutual help from one another when in need. A Cabinet minister approached me with a request to help him dismiss certain members of his extended family who had descended on him in large numbers — even his large house was not big enough to accommodate them all. An inspection by a health inspector found the house overcrowded, but not sufficiently to warrant eviction under public-health legislation. I was sorry to have to inform him that all I could offer him was my sympathy.

The minister of finance, who resided in the same area as I did, telephoned one night after 9.00 p.m. to ask me to do something about his blocked and overflowing indoor toilet, which he considered to be a public-health emergency. He did not seem to appreciate my explanation that it was a job for a plumber, so to obviate any unpleasantness I rang my chief health inspector who called at the minister's home and arranged for a plumber to come out and attend to the fault. It is of interest to note that it was not difficult to distinguish, from the street, the race of the occupant of each residence in this select area. European occupants usually had a colourful garden surrounding their houses, whereas Zambians tended to neglect the area around their houses, which looked drab by contrast.

I then received a phone call from the minister of agriculture. He was very pleasant, said it was unfortunate he had not had the pleasure of meeting me personally and invited me to have lunch with him in the city the following day. I explained that I could not accept his kind invitation because I picked up my wife each morning and we drove home to lunch. The real reason for his call then became apparent. In a smooth voice he said he did not for one moment think I would carry out our intention of taking his department to court for the sale of milk that was unfit for human consumption. The main dairy in Lusaka was administered by the Department of Agriculture, which had been warned on three occasions that unclean milk was being distributed by them as a result of a faulty bottle-washing machine. When I informed him that it was not my intention to cancel the charge against his department under the Public Health Act, he lost his charm and became distinctly unpleasant. It was eventually arranged to do away with milk bottles and the dairy installed a remarkable new Swedish machine which automatically measured a pint of milk and sealed it in a carton under hygienic conditions.

Although Zambia had been a British colony, it was the French who took most advantage of the expanding market following independence and I interviewed a number of French salesmen wishing to sell beds, blankets and other equipment we did not require in our department. However, the most prominent salesman it was my displeasure to interview was a tall, impressive-looking English gentleman. He charged into my office one day and acted as if he were doing me a favour by offering to build a completely new hospital in Lusaka, as his organization had done in other parts of the world. When I explained he had come to the wrong place and that he should interview the government Department of Health, he became annoyed because his time had been wasted and he ordered me to summon him a taxi immediately. I showed him the door leading to my secretary's office and said she could help him. He was John Stonehouse, the former Labour Party postmaster general in the UK. From his manner I had gained the impression that he was rather unstable, so was therefore not surprised to read, some time later, that he had faked his own death by leaving his clothes and belongings on a beach and then disappearing. He was later found alive and duly punished.

The Department of Health purchased many thousands of pounds worth of commodities each year, mostly motor vehicles and chemicals. All things being equal, I preferred to buy British if possible. Though these days we often hear about the decline of British industry, we were experiencing difficulty obtaining British-made products over 25 years ago. Dates of delivery were long delayed. When we placed a large order for tankers with fitted pumps for emptying septic tanks, for example, despite the assistance of the British trade commissioner, the delay in delivery became positively embarrassing. We later discovered that the firm in England had passed the order on to its factory in South Africa, which had been unable to obtain the necessary pumps.

I was fortunate in that the council arranged for me to attend the English health officers' conference each year to keep abreast with advances in public health. The conferences, which were usually held in Eastbourne, included an exhibition of public-health equipment and accessories. We were concerned about the frequent presence of insects in bread in Lusaka, despite all the bakeries having gauze-screening on the windows and double-screened doors. A well-known firm of pest control experts in England was exhibiting a new type of machine using ultraviolet light. When placed over any door or other opening into a building, it was guaranteed to exterminate all insects, including flying ants, immediately. This was the very contrivance we needed and I placed a trial order for six machines. However, when the salesman discovered that they had to be sent to Zambia, the order was declined because 'it was too much bother to pack the machines and carry out the formalities needed for the export of goods'.

On one occasion the chairman of the Health Committee accompanied me to a conference. He became very interested in mechanized refuse and sweeper vehicles and wished to purchase a number on behalf of the city council. I explained to him that with large numbers of unskilled, unemployed workers in Zambia, it would be folly to purchase these vehicles and that, in any case, it would be necessary to employ an expatriate to service them. I eventually had to seek the help of the salesman to discourage him in his eagerness to purchase the vehicles. Zambians could be successfully trained in most occupations and made good lawyers and doctors, but they were ill suited to callings that required mechanical skills. The officer in charge of the mechanical division of the RAF in Lusaka revealed to me that, with the best will in the world, they found it almost impossible to train Zambians to become efficient aircraft engineers. When Professor Dumont (a famous French colonial agronomist) visited Zambia, he advised Kaunda and his officials to improve traditional labour-intensive farming methods rather than waste money on mechanized farming machinery.

I wished to purchase a British Motor Corporation Austin car in Lusaka for my personal use. The agents, Lonrho, also acted as the agents for Mercedes Benz cars. There were a number of different models of Mercedes in the showroom, but no British cars. The salesman attempted to talk me out of buying an Austin and stressed the advantages of buying a Mercedes instead. I had to purchase my Austin by perusing illustrations in a pamphlet and waiting for delivery. We experienced the same difficulty trying to get a British Triumph car for my wife at another garage. It was depressing trying to purchase British manufactured goods abroad during the latter part of the 1960s, for British cars were gradually disappearing from the streets of Lusaka to be replaced by German, French, Italian and Japanese models.

I was amused by our cook's political standpoint. He was vehement in his dislike of Kaunda — whom he deprecated for his display of power and wealth when driving through the city in his Rolls-Royce with white-coated police motorcycle escorts — and enthusiastically supported Harry Nakambula, the leader of the opposition. One afternoon I heard a commotion going on in the backyard of our house and went out to ascertain the reason for the fracas. Two young members of the UNIP youth league were demanding to see our cook's UNIP card. I had to intervene because when he told them that he did not belong to UNIP and would refuse to pay to become a card-holding member, they threatened to manhandle him. To save himself a lot of trouble the cook reluctantly allowed me to pay the few shillings (*ngwee*) to obtain a party card on his behalf and this settled the unreasonable demand. Such were the political shenanigans of the time!

The Ford Foundation embarked on a number of useful projects in Zambia, including a scheme to employ various expatriate experts to advise government departments on how to organize and carry out their functions. My wife was asked to do confidential secretarial work each morning for one of its representatives. She worked for him in a central government building which the public, including myself, were not allowed to enter. To this day I am not fully aware of the nature of her secret work, but I suspect it was something to do with advice to the Cabinet. The Ford Foundation also offered unlimited financial aid and advice on birth control to our department in the council. This was gratefully received, but I have to admit we were unable to make much headway in our attempts either to introduce birth control to Zambian women or to encourage them to use it. Like Catholics, who actively opposed our birth-control propaganda, Zambians had a spiritual dislike of the whole idea of it and refused to take the contraceptive pill. They also saw it as a European conspiracy to prevent the increase of the African population.

Zambians in Lusaka had a strange habit of failing to attend parties or receptions to which they had been invited by Europeans (or their organizations), even although in most cases they had accepted the invitation. A young university lecturer who lived next door to us was very upset when he arranged a large party at his house, mostly for his Zambian friends and colleagues, and nearly all his guests failed to turn up. We were invited to the gathering and felt very sorry for him — all the food and drinks he had prepared were wasted. We experienced this behaviour on a number of occasions. We were therefore interested to overhear the American ambassador asking his secretary to phone the guests before dinner to remind them to come to a dinner party we were attending at the American Embassy! We were never able to ascertain whether this was an organized expression of non-cooperation or merely a lapse of memory!

We were invited to a wedding reception at a leading Lusaka hotel and were surprised and impressed by the high standard it attained — it was like a typical upper-middle-class wedding in an English town. In their deportment and dress, the bride, groom and entourage were reminiscent of a wealthy English family. This included the bride's family at the top table, the speakers, and the decorum and atmosphere of the whole occasion, which took the form of a tea party. This event, as well as often seeing expensively-dressed Zambian women buying luxurious foreign food and drink at the city's two supermarkets, where delicacies like tinned French snails, shellfish and expensive liqueurs were eagerly acquired, gave one the impression that Zambia had arrived to take its place among the advanced Western democracies, but in reality the conspicuous consumption applied only to very few Zambian families.

We were invited to another wedding deep in the countryside, away from the main road nearly 100 miles from Lusaka. A member of my community development staff was getting married and the acting head of the section insisted we attend the wedding. It turned out to be one of the most interesting days of our stay in Lusaka. In a large Roman Catholic church in the village in which the wedding was celebrated, my wife and I were the only two non-Zambians present. Following the ceremony the bride and groom, dressed in full European-style wedding dress and dark suit, received guests in a mud hut. The reception was held later in the village hall, where we were regaled with roast chicken and rice and European beer. The other guests had similar food but were served African beer. All the guests were expected to place cash or a wedding gift in a large receptacle provided for the purpose. It was a happy, friendly, enjoyable occasion and we did not feel at all isolated. Seeing the now dilapidated residence of the old district officer, with its attractive overgrown garden and tennis court, filled us with nostalgia, especially since the Zambian who had replaced him was rather pompous and unsociable. This had been an exceptional opportunity to mix with Zambians in their own environment, an experience not often available to Lusaka's European residents.

While my son was a student at Cambridge University, his economics tutor paid a visit to Zambia. Though comparatively unrecognized in England at the time, in a developing African country his views on economics were eagerly sought. We entertained him to dinner and at one point I happened to remark that there were large numbers of expatriates working in the Zambian government's Ministry of Finance, which did not seem to be economic to me. His only reply was, 'Wait until you get back to England. Then you will really see overemployment and incompetence.' This was not the first time we had heard such views expressed about contemporary conditions in England, but we somehow tended to disregard depressing stories about incompetence in the old country because they were beyond our belief.

By now I had spent over 30 years in Central Africa attending to sick Africans and Europeans as clinic or hospital patients. Most of my endeavours had been directed towards the more numerous African patients and, on reflection, I considered I had sufficient experience to express a meaningful point of view on the differences between the two races when they were indisposed.

There is no scientific evidence to support the opinion expressed by uninformed Europeans (or even by a well-known psychologist in England) that the mental capacity of Africans is inferior to that of Europeans. My medical colleagues in Salisbury — Mr Levy the neurological surgeon, Dr Gelfand the physician, and other authorities who were interested in this field of enquiry — were all agreed that there was no evidence to show that African brains are in any way inferior. Any self-evident dissimilarities are due to environmental differences, diet, or lack of opportunity.

Although biologically human beings are all close to one another, the physiques of my African male patients were, with exceptions, noticeably different from those of the Europeans. The Africans were mainly employed in heavy physical labour and because of this (their way of life and diet) they showed prominent muscular development in the limbs and torso. This may also be congenital and would account for the ascendancy of blacks in sporting activities, for becoming dominant in sports such as boxing and athletics. The European patients tended to develop protuberant abdomens with advancing age.

175

Despite my long experience with Africans I have to admit that my understanding of their psyche is rudimentary. Their natural reticence to talk about themselves, problems of communicating through interpreters and their tendency to answer questions with replies they think will please the enquirer made it difficult to get to know them well. I nonetheless became aware that many were influenced by so-called spirits and that some had visions of elves and other unlikely phenomena.

These transcendental experiences of the more unsophisticated Africans are of interest to note. They had visions of *stukwan*s (elves) and it was not unusual for a patient to present himself at the outpatient department in a condition of shock with multiple bruises, scratches and cuts. He would say he had injured himself running into trees and bushes while being pursued by *stukwan*s. These elves usually appeared while the African was riding his bicycle, which he would then abandon as he ran into the bush chased by *stukwan*s. When I first encountered this type of complaint I made the serious error of trying to explain to the sufferer that there was no such thing as a *stukwan* and that it was all in the mind. The reply, through an interpreter, was indignant and suggested there was something wrong with a doctor who disbelieved his explanation of how he had received his injuries. At first I treated the complaint by giving the patient an intravenous anaesthetic and then, when he was semiconscious, having the medical orderly shout into his ear that 'There is no such thing as a *stukwan* and all is well'. This was successful in only one or two cases. Later I referred them to the local *nganga* (witch doctor) who was a young female. She managed to cure them all, though whether by psychological means or by giving them one of her nostrums, I was never able to ascertain.

European psychology is, however, even more complicated and difficult to comprehend fully. Some Europeans are convinced they see ghosts or extraterrestrial objects, that they are influenced by 'what the stars foretell', or, as in Ireland, that there are fairies or leprechauns at the bottom of the garden.

In general, the races would contract the same infectious diseases, though the severity of their symptoms would vary according to their dissimilar states of immunity, as described in such complaints as tuberculosis, measles and poliomyelitis. The Africans were on the whole less sophisticated than the Europeans. Their lives were less complicated and consequently they experienced fewer stresses and strains. This is important because the absence of stress is often the key to good health — hence the numerous advertisements in newspapers and magazines for yoga, acupuncture, hypnotherapy and psychotherapy placing so much emphasis on their ability to combat stress. The Africans' comparative freedom from stress and anxiety meant that they experienced fewer psychosomatic complaints than their European counterparts; in other words they were less prone to those diseases in which the mind, fears and desires play a part. For example, after a serious quarrel with her husband, a European wife might well visit her general practitioner with a physical complaint, such as indigestion. Estimates differ, but it is thought that about half of all cases attending European clinics present with complaints that are psychosomatic in origin. The incidences of psychotic conditions, such as schizophrenia, were similar for both races.

Acute appendicitis was fairly common in the European community and on average I performed about one appendectomy each month. The entire time I was in Africa I saw only one case of acute appendicitis in a non-European and that was in a successful African businessman who had adopted a European way of life, including the diet. I did not see a single case of muscular sclerosis in any person born in Africa, black or white! The only cases I ever accounted were among recent immigrants from the United Kingdom.

It is difficult to compare the incidences of cancer in the two races. Statistics were not available and the majority of elderly Africans lived and died in their villages. In my own experience I found that cancer was more prevalent in the European community, with one notable exception. This was cancer of the oesophagus, or gullet, which was unexpectedly common in the African community. The geography department at the university later discovered that all the cases were from the eastern province of Zambia, where they had all imbibed a home-distilled type of Nubian gin.

There were a few complaints that were not common to both communities. As I mentioned previously, malnutrition was found in young African children who developed kwashiorkor. African adults also frequently developed chronic ulcers of the legs, known as tropical ulcers. And, with the exception of traumatic surgery, the most common operation carried out on Africans was the repair of abdominal hernias.

Many years ago when I was a student working in the outpatient department of a large London hospital, the medical officer in charge told us that if an over-dressed young man appeared with very pointed brown shoes and was hesitant about describing his symptoms, he should be offered a transfer card to the venereal disease department to avoid any further embarrassment. This proved to be sound advice. After I had been in Africa for a short while, when a young male patient arrived at the clinic and curtly said '*scop en msana*' pointing to his head and abdomen suggesting that he had a headache and abdominal discomfort, I would instantly reply, '*promiso lo brocke*' (pull down your trousers) and would be disappointed if a florid case of venereal disease was not revealed. The patient did not resent the examination, but with their keen African sense of humour would take it as a joke and invariably laughed outright.

Obstetric differences were difficult to evaluate, for only abnormal cases would be brought to our attention. Because some African women had small pelvises, usually due to rickets in childhood, cases of blocked labour were regularly admitted to the hospital. If the application of forceps failed, the baby would be delivered by a Caesarean section. It is difficult to believe this, but if a baby had not been born by the expected time, it was the practice in the villages for a strong man to place a leather thong or strap around the top of the mother's abdomen and pull with all his strength in the hope that the baby would be delivered. When such cases arrived at the hospital almost moribund it was difficult to save both the mother and the child. A retained afterbirth was a common complication following the birth of a baby. Its manual removal became a routine procedure and the fear of infection was dismissed with the introduction of antibiotic drugs.

Apart from the obstetric cases, large numbers of patients were admitted to the hospital in a moribund condition. This situation was caused either by difficulties and delays in getting transport to the hospital, or, in some cases, by a patient's initial treatment by an *nganga* having gone wrong. This was what accounted for the widespread belief that hospitals were places of death.

It should be appreciated that all the medical episodes I describe took place in Central Africa during the 1940s, 1950s and 1960s and that circumstances have changed considerably during the intervening 30-odd years. With the advent of independence in the territories, many more citizens have become educated and an African middle class has emerged. The archetype of a patient is therefore different — diets have been improved, transport has been made easier, hospitals and clinics have improved their facilities, and many more consultants in the various disciplines have been appointed.

My extended contract with Lusaka City Council was drawing to an end and we were busy making arrangements to sell our household goods and send what possessions we considered worthwhile to the United Kingdom, where I had already been appointed as a deputy MOH in an English county. At the time it was difficult and expensive to transport goods by sea, so we had to send our belongings by air freight.

Our domestic servants seemed concerned about our impending departure. Our old cook, who acted as spokesman, said, 'We cannot understand why you wish to leave Zambia when you seem to be so happy here. We want *Unshlungu* [Europeans] to stay here and not leave us in despair.' He then enquired, 'Who will do your housework and especially who will clean your shoes when you live in England?' When I replied, 'My wife will do the housework and I will clean my own shoes,' he shook his head, laughed and intimated that he did not believe one word I had said.

We left Lusaka on a sunny morning between Christmas 1970 and the New Year. We were travelling by bus to Salisbury, where we had business to transact, and would fly back to England from there. The bus left from a central Lusaka hotel at midday and a number of our friends came to have a departing drink and to see us off. It was a happy farewell. We realized that this would be our last journey out of Zambia (or the old Northern Rhodesia we knew so well) and felt sentimental as we passed through the familiar streets of Lusaka on our way south. We had spent many

179

happy years in the country and the last four in Lusaka had been both interesting and rewarding. As we departed I at least had the satisfaction of knowing that the city health department I had helped develop and was now leaving was comprehensive and well-organized. The journey to Salisbury, where we arrived that evening, was comfortable and pleasant. The bus driver was an educated Rhodesian African and we noted that he tuned the radio news to the BBC and not to the Rhodesian Broadcasting System. We left Salisbury for London on a British Airways flight two days later.

7

England

We arrived in England on the last day of 1970 in a dense fog. The aircraft captain announced that we may possibly have to land at Prestwick because of the poor visibility over the south of England, but the next bulletin stated that we were about to land at Heathrow and, as we were unable to see anything in the fog, I presume he made an uneventful instrument landing. Despite the inclement weather we were glad to be in England once again. The soft, garden-like countryside, which can only be seen in this part of the world, even in winter, was a decided attraction. After a few weeks' temporary residence in a hotel, we moved into our home, which we had purchased five years previously. It had been let to the United States Air Force, which had an air base nearby. It was not long before we settled down to our new life deep in the glorious countryside of rural Essex. We appreciated the radio which made listening worthwhile, the newspapers which were worth reading and the television programmes, which were vastly superior to any we had seen in any other country we had visited or lived in, made worthwhile viewing.

I commenced my employment as a deputy MOH in a populous area of a large county in early 1971, and had to drive for over 20 miles from my home to my place of work, across country, each day. Remembering the forewarnings of our English visitors to Lusaka, I soon discovered that English attitudes had changed markedly since I had last worked there over 30 years previously. There was an air of discontent in the general demeanour of our large office staff, whose work was uninspired. Their timekeeping was appalling. Like myself, they were due to commence work at 9.00 a.m., but it would be about 9.20 a.m. before the last office employee turned up to work.

There is a dictum which states that 'comparisons are odious', but one inevitably and instinctively compares the working and living conditions of a country in which one has settled with those of the country (or countries) one has recently left. From the onset I was unimpressed with the standard of public-health administration in England. Perhaps my expectations were too high, for when I had left the old country over 30 years previously, the United Kingdom was considered a world leader in the practice of public health.

A few days after I began working in the area I had occasion to visit what had been described as 'the leading men's barber shop in the town' for a haircut. It would be an understatement to say that the establishment was filthy and unhygienic. The hair of many previous customers lay on the floor in a deep layer. The same dirty plastic sheet was used to cover the upper halves of all customers, and the same unsterilized brush and comb were used on a communal basis on all patrons. On my return to my office I asked the chief health officer to inspect the premises and warn the owner to adopt more hygienic practices in his shop and, if necessary, to prosecute him for contravening the hairdressers' regulations under the Public Health Act. To my amazement the health officer had to admit that hairdressers' regulations had not been promulgated as by-laws by our local authority, so that there was no law under which hairdressers could be prosecuted under the Public Health Act. In Lusaka city centre, in accordance with local by-laws, each patron visiting a barber shop had to be supplied with a clean laundered covering and neck towel, and all brushes and combs had to be sterilized before use on each customer.

A short while later I went into a high-class public house, where I ordered ham sandwiches and a beer for lunch. I was reading my newspaper and was in the act of conveying a sandwich to my mouth when it was grabbed out of my hand by a large Alsatian dog. When I told the publican what had happened and said that it was illegal to keep dogs on premises where food was served, he rudely suggested I mind my own business because the dogs were kept in the pub for security reasons! I did mind my own business and once again asked the chief health officer to warn the publican not to keep dogs in his public house. This resulted in a letter from a firm of solicitors in Birmingham, representing the Licensed Victuallers' Association, indirectly accusing us of objecting to a blind man entering a bar with his guide dog! When I decided to resign from my appointment over a year later, correspondence in relation to this incident was still going on. These two illustrations of the difficulties encountered in the administration of public health in England both occurred during my first few weeks in the department; I could give many more examples of more serious and complicated cases in which I was involved. I do not wish to infer that we were in any way inferior to any other local authority health department, but somehow there was a general deterioration in the conduct of affairs in the United Kingdom. I often cogitated on how much easier it would be if only we had the same law we had in Zambia whereby any person or organization producing or handling food or drink for human consumption had to be licensed annually by the MOH.

Our personal health division was well developed and efficient. We employed large numbers of health visitors, district nurses and clinic nurses; we also ran many public-health clinics and were responsible for providing old-age homes. As in Lusaka, the department was also in charge of social services, for which we largely employed retired policemen, who incidentally made excellent social workers.

The town in which my headquarters were located had what in England is described as a large coloured community. I was not aware of any racial problems, but after attending frequent public-health clinics became cognizant of the conspicuous differences between Asian and African mothers. It was most likely because of their country of origin that the African mothers all spoke English, dressed like local mothers and, in effect, could be described as black Englishwomen. The Asian women, by comparison, hardly ever spoke any English, dressed in Eastern-style garments, and did not in any respect appear to have become assimilated, even if they had been resident in England for many years. In general, the Asian residents preserved their own culture and identity with regard to dress, religion and diet. This necessitated the nursing staff having to become familiar with their lifestyle in order to advise them adequately on maternal and infant welfare.

Pupil midwives were trained in the department and one of my duties was to instruct them on matters relating to public health. I was surprised to find only one European in the class of six pupils. I took advantage of the opportunity to discuss birth control with them and pointed out that they were in a unique position to carry out birth-control propaganda because mothers who had recently conceived were more susceptible to birth-control indoctrination. I spoke about large families exacerbating poverty and starvation in developing countries and about how the world was becoming over populated. When enquiring about their attitude to birth control I was taken aback when they admitted that they were opposed to all forms of birth control because, as I had heard so often before in Africa, 'it was a European conspiracy to prevent an increase in the black population and, furthermore, African families required more children to look after their parents in old age'.

Our health department served five different rural and urban councils and this necessitated my spending an inordinate amount of time attending committee and council meetings. I therefore had the redoubtable opportunity of contacting local government politicians and town clerks *en masse*. Over the years I have served a very conservative council in Rhodesia, a black non-political council in Zambia, and Labour, Conservative as well as non-political councils in England. The first observation I have to make is that there is little difference between the various councils, whether black, white, red or blue. I would sometimes suddenly wake up from a state of semiconsciousness during a long, boring committee meeting and have to remind myself that I was in England and not in Zambia, for the subject matter and jargon were so similar. After many years of associating with politicians I am personally convinced that they are born and not made. I do not know what induces certain individuals to seek power over their fellow men, but politicians, who come from all classes in society, from professional men to labourers, nearly all have this instinct. They are mostly populist extroverts, conscious of their own importance and seeking publicity in the hope of becoming a celebrated public figure. Some councillors were genuine, altruistic individuals who sought election in order to look after the interests of their electorate, but they were in the minority!

Academics who have studied and know about philosophy, economics and politics rarely embark on political careers. It is unfortunate that few politicians, to my knowledge, have studied the Acts of 1872 and 1888, which established the modern local authorities and which suggested that councillors should be retired, responsible individuals, willing to look after the interests of the residents living in their neighbourhood and without any financial or other 'axes to grind'. It was not anticipated that they would develop into party political organizations. Recent genetics research suggests that everything we take upon ourselves is predetermined, so it is likely that most politicians have a defective gene that makes them wish to seek power over their fellow citizens and keen to attend committee meetings! There seems to be little difference between local and central government politicians and many local authority legislators eventually seek election to central government. Politicians (and politics in general) have only recently become unpopular among the population at large and I wonder why it has taken so long. The hypocrisy of Labour and Conservative councillors, who criticize and abuse one another in council meetings and are then the best of friends at a council reception to entertain some prominent visitor, is contemptible. They are all politicians first and political opponents second. This is exemplified in the House of Commons when members of all political parties vote in harmony and good grace when they have occasion to vote in support of a rise in their own remuneration!

Town clerks, now referred to as chief administration officers, worked in close contact with councillors and, in my experience, were an unhelpful lot. They were usually lawyers by profession who equivocated and rarely gave a direct answer to any query. And, as the following incident illustrates, they had a well-developed sense of their own importance. I had received a report from an MOH in Newcastle that a number of residents in an old-age home had suffered from severe gastroenteritis after eating pork pies prepared at a bacon factory in our area. An inspection showed that the kitchen was staffed by a number of mentally-deficient girls from a nearby institution. We agreed, with the help of a health inspector, to educate them about hygienic cooking methods, but a few weeks later the MOH of a south coast resort phoned to say that a large number of boys at a public school in his area had severe diarrhoea and vomiting after eating pig products from the same factory. The cooperative young manager of the factory agreed to close the kitchen permanently and I thought the matter had been resolved. However, it was not long before I received a call from the town clerk enquiring if I had closed the above-mentioned kitchen. When I replied in the affirmative he brusquely informed me that I did not have the authority to close the kitchen and that it had been my duty to report the matter to him who, in turn, would have applied to a magistrate to carry out the closure. And, what was more important, I was personally responsible for any loss due to the closure of the kitchen, perhaps amounting to hundreds of pounds each day! I did not tell him that the closure was carried out voluntarily by the management!

It was at about this juncture that our department received a circular letter from the Department of Health and Social Services, then under the authority of Secretary for Health Keith Joseph, the government minister largely responsible for Mrs Thatcher's promotion to prime minister. The letter stated that hospitals were being inefficiently managed through a failure to apply proper business methods and that, in future, accountants, or people with similar skills, would be appointed as hospital managers! As a former superintendent of a hospital abroad, the very idea of a non-medical superintendent filled me with scepticism. Medical staff sometimes needed to be disciplined for upsetting the smooth routine of the hospital organization and I could not imagine an accountant or other bureaucrat telling a physician or surgeon what he or she should or should not do! My incredulity was recently justified when a hospital pathologist misdiagnosed hundreds of specimens of cancer cells and was not reprimanded for months, even years, despite her fellow consultants being aware of her faulty work.

The difficulties I encountered in completing any undertaking and the indifferent disposition of the staff did not make working as a deputy MOH in an English county the most interesting or stimulating period of my medical career. I therefore resigned my appointment after less than two years' service. I demoted myself by applying for (and obtaining) the post of district MOH and schools medical officer in the area in which I was resident. This meant I did not have to travel so far to work each day.

However, after a few years I became bored — most of my work consisted of giving routine examinations to babies and school children and injecting babies with prophylactic vaccines, which should have been done by health visitors or other qualified nursing staff — and so retired completely. It is worth mentioning that shortly afterwards local authority health departments in England were abolished and a Department of Social Services was established. Health officers become responsible for environmental health and the MOH was replaced by a central government-employed community health officer.

My time in full retirement was taken up with gardening, fishing and occasional shooting on our own property, but it was less pleasant than I had anticipated because I missed the lack of mental stimulation. I was therefore not sorry when our local medical practitioner in the next village approached me to join his practice as a part-time medical assistant. I agreed to work with him for three days each week and on alternate weekends.

It was agreeable to be back in harness once again, especially since we had an amicable relationship and worked well together, but I soon found that general practice in England was completely different from the same occupation as practised in Broken Hill or Livingstone. It lacked the sense of excitement and responsibility I had experienced in Central Africa, where all patients requiring hospital investigation or admission continued to be treated by the general practitioner and where specialist help was infrequently sought because of inaccessibility.

In England we were not permitted to care for our patients in hospital and transferred all our most interesting cases to an appropriate consultant — we were merely the distributors of the seriously ill. It was, however, gratifying to come into contact with patients and to become involved in their troubles. The majority of my patients had psychosomatic complaints and usually expected to be treated with some drug they imagined would cure their ills. They would be disappointed, even hostile, if a prescription for a particular drug, such as penicillin for a viral sore throat, was refused on the grounds that I considered it unnecessary or, indeed, harmful. In Africa the non-European patients were less likely to be troubled by psychosomatic diseases and preferred to be treated by drugs given by injection rather than by mouth. They were also more fatalistic in their approach to ill health.

It was not long before I was asked to take a third share of the practice in which we were working. This would mean that the NHS, rather than the practice employing me as a medical assistant, would pay my salary. I had no desire to join the NHS, but, following protracted exhortation, I finally agreed to accept the arrangement provided I did not have to deal with any administrative matters between the NHS and ourselves.

My reason for not wishing to join the NHS was that it is a large cumbersome organization administered by non-medical personnel. However, and perhaps even more important to me, was the fact that I had come to realize during my short time as a local medical practitioner that most consultants only worked part time in NHS hospitals and treated private patients in the same hospitals in which they were appointed.

Some of my patients with chronic debilitating complaints, such as an arthritic hip joint, had to wait months or even years to be admitted to hospital for surgical treatment, but for those with the financial means to pay for their treatment, the operation would be performed at the same hospital in a matter of days or weeks. This meant that there was a two-tier system of medical attention based on a patient's ability to pay.

Throughout my career in Africa, I personally, as well as all my colleagues in the railways, government and local authority medical services, had always worked to the best of our ability on a salaried basis. Though we were permitted to engage in private practice, this was usually negligible and in remote areas.

Aneurin Bevan, the minister responsible for the creation of the National Health Service, had wanted to introduce a full-time salaried medical service in the United Kingdom, but this idea was strongly opposed by the medical profession at the time. There is no doubt that the majority of patients would have benefited from everyone being treated solely on the basis of their medical requirements without any financial considerations being taken into account.

Unhappily my senior partner, who was much younger than myself, died suddenly and the practice automatically became my responsibility. I was not pleased about the turn of events, but managed to arrange for his son, who was also in the medical profession, to take over the practice.

We were eventually appointed as the police surgeons in our district and also as the medical officers for the United States Air Force base situated in our locality. We were extremely fortunate that our practice, which consisted of two country general practitioners, should have been chosen to serve the American base where many hundreds of air force personnel and their families were stationed. It enhanced our profile considerably.

For the next ten years I spent my mornings seeing local patients in our surgery and most of my afternoons seeing American patients at the base clinic. There were some marked differences between the English and American patients; the latter were less restrained, friendlier and noisier than their English counterparts. Their appearance and dress were also different and a large proportion of the females were very obese. I had no difficulty communicating with them on a one-to-one basis, despite their different accent and colloquial speech, but if they were conversing among themselves it sounded as if they were speaking a foreign language and I would be unable to follow the conversation.

From the outset I had a unique opportunity to observe race relations as practised in the United States Air Force. There were more or less equal numbers of blacks and whites at the base and there was absolutely no suggestion of racism. Senior officers may have been black and junior airmen white, but they all mixed and worked as equals within the confines of their ranks. As they all wore the same uniform, were of the same educational standard and had similar accents, after a while I stopped noticing the colour of the skin of the patient I was examining. This should have served as a lesson for the Royal Air Force and Army where, I was informed, there were no non-European commissioned officers. However, despite my experience of colour blindness at the base, I would automatically notice the presence of any black person in our village and wonder what he or she were doing there. On reflection I now believe that this is the basis of unthinking, unreasonable, unconscious racial prejudice.

As was usual for a general practice, we held two surgeries each weekday, one in the morning and one in the evening, with up to 15 patients being seen at each session. As stated before, this usually meant seeing a patient with some minor complaint such as a sore throat or rash, having a short discussion about their trouble, issuing a prescription and calling 'next please'. Only occasionally did we see a patient with a more serious complaint that required a thorough interrogation and examination. The time between surgeries was spent visiting patients in their homes, doing insurance or other routine examinations and attending to correspondence. Nevertheless, our association with the American base and our work as police surgeons made our practice more rewarding and interesting than most.

Police duties were not generally popular among practitioners because they could be burdensome and involved a large amount of night work. In our case we had to travel 11 miles to the police station each time we were called out. Because these were the days before breathalysers were in common use, most of our police work consisted of taking specimens for analysis from drivers suspected of having excessive alcohol in their blood, usually in the middle of the night. We also had to examine prisoners and police personnel who had been injured in a violent confrontation. It was amazing how little the general public knew about the young lawless riffraff who congregated in the streets of town centres after the public houses had closed late on a summer's night. The police were often attacked without provocation and it became impossible for them to patrol alone at night. They had to go out in pairs or even larger numbers. I have to admit that I was nervous driving through the streets where these louts congregated. On one occasion I noticed three of them approaching my car when I had stopped at a traffic light and quickly accelerated through the red light.

I thought that the police were too tolerant with these young criminals. They were efficient in their unenviable occupation, but remarks such as 'I know him personally and he is not such a bad chap. It is only when he has had too much to drink that he goes berserk' really annoyed me because I do not consider drunkenness an excuse for criminal behaviour.

The police surgeon would also become involved in cases of lawbreaking by psychiatrically disturbed individuals who had been allowed back into the community because the government, in its wisdom, had decided to close down the mental institutions. These were formidable cases to handle because it was very difficult to get them readmitted to mental hospitals as voluntary patients. In the course of their duties many policemen proved to be conscientious social workers; in fact they were sometimes more effective than the social workers themselves.

I was involved in three cases of rape during the period of my service as a police surgeon in England and could recollect three other cases of the same crime among the European community during my service as a police surgeon in Rhodesia. On investigation not one of these cases turned out to be genuine. Two of the victims were deeply religious women who had been willing to share a bed with the accused, but when the sexual act became inevitable had scrambled out of the bed and rushed out of the room shouting rape. It is probably coincidental that all the European cases of rape in which I was involved turned out to be authentic.

Crimes among the African population in Rhodesia were different from those committed by Europeans in either Rhodesia or England. Instances of assault were far more frequent and more serious in the African population. Knives were commonly used in inflicting bodily harm with intent to kill and prosecutions for murder were not infrequent. The odd case of rape for which I had to give evidence were nearly always instances of a lone female being attacked as she was walking through the bush, where her cries for help went unheard.

An aspect of general practice that did not appeal to me was the established custom of interviewing drug salesmen who offered all sorts of inducements to practitioners to use their particular brand of drug. Payment was offered to use their drug in the treatment of patients on a trial basis. They usually brought small gifts, such as fountain pens, torches or personal stationery, and we were invited to luncheon or dinner parties at expensive restaurants. After a while I refused to see drug salesmen, but was made to feel that this was an unusual and unfriendly attitude to adopt. A dispensing practice (which most country practices were) derived a large part of its income from dispensing drugs and some of the methods adopted by doctors and drug companies were questionable. Certain drug companies were willing to supply more drugs than were ordered.

As I had now reached the eighth decade of my being, I decided to retire permanently and was given a memorable farewell party by the practice. In retrospect, I was not sorry to retire because the profession I was leaving was no longer the honourable one I had entered more than 60 years previously. Like other institutions in the UK, medicine had become commercially orientated, no doubt under the influence of a government whose prime minister had openly stated that 'there is no such thing as society' and had stressed the misconception that profit should be the spur. Gone were the days when we were so absorbed in our work as medical practitioners in Africa that financial considerations were rarely mentioned.

The average medical practitioner nowadays is more interested in building bigger and better surgeries with government grants and in other financial advantages than in interesting medical conditions. Hospitals have been turned into competing business institutions to which patients gain access more easily if their general practitioners are fundholders and therefore able to pay for their treatment. Whereas fundholding medical practices have been granted extra financial aid by the government to pay for their patients' admittance to hospital, those under the care of a doctor who is not in a fundholding practice have far more difficulty gaining admission to hospital. With financial considerations dominating the service instead of the medical needs of the patient (which should be the only consideration when someone is unwell), the National Health Service, once the envy of the world, is now in danger of disintegrating.

Financially, the NHS is a bottomless pit and its survival will depend on an appraisal of how to curb expenditure. When I was the medical superintendent of a large infectious diseases hospital, with hundreds of beds, in what was then Rhodesia, apart from domestic and cleaning workers, the only non-medical staff employed in the hospital were one clerk and one typist, and we managed very well. In those days hospitals were efficiently managed by medical superintendents and matrons. The present situation in the NHS is unrealistic. The countless millions of pounds spent on unnecessary so-called administrators, who, according to a recent official statement, spent £73,000,000 last year on their car allowances alone, could be saved by the drastic reduction of their numbers, and the money spent on patient care, which after all is the object of the service.

The MOH in Salisbury, Rhodesia, was asked to support the director of medical services' campaign not to allow a heart transplant surgeon to work in government hospitals in the territory. A young Rhodesian-born doctor had been trained as a heart transplant surgeon in the United States of America and he wished to settle in his home town and continue with his heart transplant surgical practice. The director of medical services rightly pointed out that operating theatre and nurses' time, the use of hospital beds and the cost of very expensive drugs were not justified when there were virtually thousands of patients awaiting hernia operations. Despite the opposition of the government, city council and public, who are emotional about transplant operations because of the coverage they have received in the media, we were eventually successful in persuading the young heart surgeon to settle in a more prosperous environment.

Other than kidney transplants, which save money because they make dialysis unnecessary, each transplant operation costs the NHS £20,000 and the time may come when these expensive procedures may have to be excluded from the NHS while thousands of patients are awaiting hip or knee transplants, or other more mundane surgical procedures to relieve their pain and discomfort. The financing of more expensive surgery could be undertaken by private or charitable organizations.

The NHS is being turned into a series of monolithic competitive businesses run by managers and accountants. The influences of medical personnel, nursing staff and medical auxiliaries are being usurped and this trend is permeating all aspects of medical practice in England.

193

8

Zimbabwe Interludes

We have visited Zimbabwe, formerly Rhodesia, on three occasions since it was made independent under a majority-rule government in 1980. In the intervening ten years between leaving Central Africa in 1970 and independence, as predicted an escalating bush war ensued in which the Rhodesian Army and Air Force were unable to defeat the nationalist guerrillas. Following a cease-fire in 1979 a constitutional conference was held at Lancaster House in London. This resulted in a British-supervised election in Rhodesia, in which all races participated and which ensured the election of a black government led by Robert Mugabe.

Because we only spent a short time there, about two to three weeks on each occasion, and were there merely as visitors, I do not feel I can justifiably express any authoritative opinions about the changes that have taken place since independence. On each occasion we have visited the territory we have been struck by how little has changed in the interim. Harare, previously known as Salisbury, remains as clean and as pleasant as it ever was. Standards in hotels, restaurants and bars are still equivalent to those found in Europe. In brief, Zimbabwe has been sustained as a modern country with civilized standards and principles. It was noticeable that some organizations were still being controlled by an occasional European in the background, such as a hotel manager.

Our old friends still resident in Harare appeared to be contented and, without exception, had not had any serious complaints since the advent of majority government. It soon became evident that the Africans in Zimbabwe had no desire to revenge the oppressive treatment they had endured under previous, mainly European, minority governments. Law and order, in common with most other countries, had broken down to a certain extent, especially with regard to burglaries, and a number of householders in the more expensive lush suburbs either had high security walls built around their properties or employed night watchmen.

Well-dressed young African couples attending banquets and other functions were conspicuous as they arrived in the inevitable Mercedes, with liveried chauffeur, at the hotel where we usually stayed in Harare. Years later Doris Lessing, in her book *African Laughter*, describes these types as the 'chefs' who were largely responsible for the bribery and corruption which was prevalent in the country. Like many Zimbabwean residents, she wondered why Prime Minister Mugabe had not adopted any measures to deal with these young politicians or government servants who had advanced so rapidly following independence.

We were surprised and disappointed to observe that certain arrogant Europeans continued to treat Africans in the same discourteous manner they had before the advent of a black government. We were staying at a hotel in Inyanga, a beautiful mountainous holiday resort reminiscent of Scotland in the sun, when I inadvertently left my car lights on and the battery was flat the following morning. The hotel handyman — a large, brusque, old-style Rhodesian — arrived in his Land-Rover accompanied by a young African assistant. He ordered his assistant to fix the battery leads from his Land-Rover to my car in a harsh manner and called him a stupid idiot when he did not connect the leads quickly enough for his liking. I asked him how he managed to treat Africans in this abusive manner now that there was a black government in power. His astonishing reply was, 'This crowd are incapable of running the country and we, the Europeans, still run the outfit so I carry on as usual.'

Two nights later, in a hotel bar in the same district, we heard a couple of Europeans loudly abusing and condemning Africans in no uncertain terms. My wife and I were embarrassed by their opinions, but the African barman showed no sign of taking exception to their disparaging remarks. On another occasion a friend had invited us out to dinner at a restaurant in one of the suburbs. We noted that all the waitresses and other workers in the restaurant were Europeans. The proprietor informed us that he would not have a black working in his restaurant because they were dishonest and incompetent. The position was so incongruous that we left wondering why the owner preferred to live in an independent African country. We were astonished that the bad behaviour of their white denigrators did not bring about a response from the Africans concerned. Perhaps it was because they were conditioned to the status quo, despite the change in government!

While staying in Inyanga we visited the Pungwe Gorge on the Mozambique border, an exceptional beauty spot where nature had endowed the surrounding countryside with magnificent views, especially of a stream winding its way through a deep gorge far below our vantage point. It took the whole morning to drive from Inyanga to the gorge on a little-used dirt road. An extraordinary feature of the trip was that we did not pass another vehicle or see another human being — neither did we see any wildlife, even rabbits — during the entire journey. When we had lived in that part of the world one would never proceed very far into the countryside without encountering some form of wildlife. Only a few weeks after we visited the gorge three young European tourists were murdered while viewing the panorama from the same vantage point.

On the last occasion we were in Zimbabwe we took a day-return flight from Harare to Victoria Falls. We had anticipated changes there when we boarded a large four-engined Boeing aircraft, for when we had left the falls 30 years before there had been only a small airfield for light aircraft. On arrival we noticed that a large international airport had been constructed a short distance from the falls alongside the road leading south, no longer a picturesque strip road but now a 22-foot-wide macadamized highway. Apart from the Victoria Falls Hotel, the village used to consist of a small police and customs post, a curio shop, a general store and a few huts for visitors. It now boasted another hotel, a large pretentious casino, bank, building society, numerous shops and a large tourist area where African arts and crafts were displayed and African woodcarvers and dancers performed. We had never seen presentations of local African dancing in the past and doubted their authenticity. New wide roads and paths had been constructed in the vicinity of the falls, which were artificially lit up at night. The Victoria Falls Hotel had been enlarged and modernized and, in our opinion, had lost its elegant charm. When we were stationed there the falls and the area immediately around them were left as Livingstone had discovered them and we were distressed to find all the new development. Some might see it as progress, but for us it was an appallingly retrogressive step!

While visiting Victoria Falls we had a natural desire to see Livingstone and renew contact with our old home and haunts in the town. With this in mind we hired a taxi to drive us the seven miles to Livingstone, but were incredulous when the taxi driver informed us that we may have difficulty crossing the border between Zimbabwe and Zambia. That proved to be an understatement! What had been a single wooden barrier lifted by a lone policeman who handed you a slip advising you to report to the immigration and customs department in Livingstone if you were a stranger in the area, was now a large office building where the Zimbabwe immigration and customs departments were stationed. Despite our telling them that we only wished to visit Livingstone for about an hour, we were requested to fill in large detailed forms and instructed to produce all the Zimbabwean currency we possessed, which they sealed in a packet for us to recover on our return. We were allowed to keep British currency, which we fortunately had with us. The taxi was not permitted to pass through the border and we were told we could hire another taxi on the Zimbabwean side. We then entered another even larger Zambian immigration and customs office where uniformed officials curtly asked us to fill in more forms giving full details about ourselves. They informed us there were no taxis available there and we would have to phone and order one from Livingstone. Their attitude was so abrupt and unpleasant that we had had enough and decided to give up the attempt to visit Livingstone. Believe it or not, the official on the Zimbabwean side was annoyed when we returned to reclaim our money because, he

197

said, 'we had wasted his time'. While we were there a large party of tourists shepherded by a guide passed through from the Zambian to the Zimbabwean side without difficulty.

I have reported this episode in full because it illustrated how two recently independent African states, Zambia and Zimbabwe, were far less friendly than they had been in the days when they were known as Northern and Southern Rhodesia. There is an old saying that advises one not to return to one's old domicile years after having left it because the changes that have taken place may prove to be upsetting. This was certainly the case when we visited Victoria Falls and hoped to visit Livingstone.

While driving through the countryside, especially between Inyanga and Umtali, we noticed numerous round mud huts and large numbers of children along the road. They appeared to be deprived members of the community whose poverty was unmistakable. As visitors we were not in a position to comprehend the mood of the Zimbabwean people, but we were told by European residents that there was general discontent with the government because it had been unable to fulfil its promises to the people of increased prosperity and land for all who required it. They were also unhappy about the rapid rise and ostentatious affluence of a few top individuals who were suspected of being corrupt. On more than one occasion we heard the view expressed that if a general election were to be held tomorrow and Ian Smith stood as a candidate he would be elected in a constituency where the majority of electors were African. We very much doubted the validity of this prognostication.

Epilogue

I had worked in the medical profession for nearly 60 years, of which 32 years were spent in Central Africa, with a two-year break in the army in Equatorial Africa. We lived in the Dominion of South Africa during the early impressionable years of our lives and later lived and worked in the independent colony of Southern Rhodesia, the colonial territory of Northern Rhodesia, the Federation of Central Africa in Rhodesia and the independent country of Zambia. This was during an era when the sun never set on the British Empire. It was also when the colonial territories were making history by demanding, and in turn being granted, their independence. Unlike other colonial powers such as France and Holland, hardly a shot was fired in anger during the process of British decolonization.

In recent years it has become fashionable for the media to deprecate the British Colonial Empire and suggest it was created to exploit the colonial people. In my long association with the colonial administration in Northern Rhodesia and Kenya, in the course of my professional work and as a friend of numerous colonial civil servants, I saw absolutely no evidence of the local population being exploited either by the colonial administration itself or by any of the individuals working within it; and, to the best of my knowledge, this was true also of all the other colonial territories. British colonial civil servants were dedicated, relatively underpaid individuals who joined the service not only for the interesting and adventurous career opportunities it offered, but to serve and help advance the progress of the indigenous populations of the various colonial territories. They gave these underdeveloped people a sense of justice and taught them how to respect law and

199

order. They initiated and developed technical services such as health and agriculture. They governed in an honest and exemplary manner. Unlike politicians, they had 'no axe to grind' and used their professional knowledge for the benefit of the people. And because, for example, a medical man would be in charge of health, an engineer in charge of works and an educationist in charge of education, the legislative assemblies knew what they were doing. The majority of the members of the provincial administration — all trained administrators headed by the governor — could be described as quintessential English country gentlemen. Their cultured and elegant demeanour and appearance were the envy of many others and they commanded the respect of the colonial peoples.

There was exploitation in Northern Rhodesia, but this was by the large international mining companies and by the Indian traders who had a virtual monopoly of the retail shops that served Africans. The mining companies may have repatriated their profits and paid dividends to shareholders in countries other than Northern Rhodesia, but they were the main employers of labour and providers of revenue to the government. The independent government of Zambia continues to welcome their presence in the territory. Though aggressive imperialism and exploitation were the approved aims of the British people and government in the days of Rhodes at the turn of the century, this should not be confused with the situation we encountered in Northern Rhodesia many years later.

Incidentally, I have often wondered what these fine, agreeable young British gentlemen who used to join the Colonial Service in their thousands have been doing with their lives since the demise of the British Empire. One rarely meets anyone who would have been regarded as a suitable candidate for the old Colonial Service. Have they joined the growing army of stockbrokers, accountants or other paper-handling plutocrats?

Our time in Africa was interesting, exciting, compelling and entertaining, with unexpected variations which at times brought tribulations and vicissitudes, but these tended only to make it all the more exciting. In retrospect, we led a life of extreme luxury with willing, attentive servants in an acceptable environment and with protracted vacations in Europe and North America when travel was a self-indulgent pleasure. It is difficult to describe to the present generation the pleasure of luxury ocean travel in a liner on a regular voyage. It would take 21 days by express train and Royal Mail ocean liner to travel from Central Africa to London, a journey which now takes about nine hours, herded into an aircraft like sheep and served plastic food.

Having completed my long professional career of treating patients from primitive Bushmen leading nomadic lives in Bechuanaland to British patricians and foreign notables at the Victoria Falls Hotel, and latterly from English country folk and criminals to United States Air Force personnel, with all of whom I had close associations, I have become a disillusioned cynic who has lost faith in humanity. How was it possible for ordinary informed citizens to vote for the Smith government in Rhodesia when they must have been aware of the dire consequences of their action? Genghis Khan flourished as a despicable dictator in the thirteenth century. Christianity has been practised for 2000 years, there was a renaissance in the fifteenth century, and I am old enough to remember how we all thought that the First World War would be the war to end all human conflict in the future! Despite the continual increase in knowledge and understanding, a vile dictator like Hitler was elected to power in Germany in this century. Science has made steady progress and has outstripped man's ability to keep up with the benefits it has bestowed. The environment is being destroyed at an alarming rate. We have witnessed the destruction of forests and the gradual disappearance of wildlife in Central Africa and the pollution of the air and water in the more developed countries. No serious attempt is being made to control this destruction of the planet on which we live. There is a ruthless contempt for human life as evidenced by the increase in violence and the continuation of civil and religious wars in many parts of the world at the present time. Unless one happens to be a blathering politician, an odd journalist, or a believer in miracles such as the physiological impossibility of an immaculate conception, it is unreasonable to be optimistic about the future of mankind.

We live in a changing age of computerization, which is not highly regarded by senior members of society. What has happened to the England which, with all its faults, conceivably remains the most civilized and tolerant country it always was? Why has it become a nation of losers? England gave the world football, cricket and tennis, but has become unsuccessful when competing in these sports with other countries! Its manufacturing industry has been decimated. On visiting the new Canary Wharf development area in London where empty blocks of office accommodation have replaced the appealing old West and East India docks from where we used to sail to Africa at the end of our holidays, I was filled with sentimental nostalgia. I have heard it described as a monument to Thatcherism! What is more important is that Britain has lost its ability to influence world opinion, which it achieved so successfully before the dissolution of the empire.

I am unable to remember the exact date, but poll tax was discontinued in Rhodesia some time before or just after the Second Word War because it was uncollectable; it was replaced by a hut tax because, unlike individuals, huts could not move away and disappear. Mrs Thatcher and her compliant government, in all their wisdom, decided to introduce a poll tax in England in 1988 with disastrous results because it was resented by the populace and was impossible to collect! When we lived in Livingstone we were disturbed at night by the monotonous repetitive sounds of the continuous beating of drums. They were alleged, by Africans, to keep away evil spirits. In England when we turned on the radio or television we were often irritated by the similar and even more raucous repetitive sounds referred to as pop music.

Before I left England to settle in Central Africa a favourite social achievement was to be able to dance the foxtrot or waltz in which you embraced your partner closely and derived pleasure in the process. In Africa the sexes danced separately and there was no embracing of partners. On our return to the UK years later dancing had changed and the younger generation danced without close body contact. Male and female partners danced separately by twisting and turning in time to the loud repetitive sounds, but less rhythmically than they did in Africa. As I mention earlier, comparisons are said to be odious, so I shall not pursue other examples in case I am accused of suggesting that the United Kingdom is yielding to the influence of primitive Africa!

Epilogue

It is not easy to predict the future of the three independent territories in Central Africa. Historically, almost every sovereign nation in the world has been formed by violence as exemplified in Russia, Germany, England and other European nations. America had its civil war following independence, while practically all the African territories have had (or are having) civil wars or have become military dictatorships since independence, irrespective of which colonial power granted them self-government. Angola and Mozambique, which were so recently engulfed in civil wars, were Portuguese colonial territories. Violence erupted in Zaire where Belgium had been the colonial power, civil war in Somaliland where Italy had been the colonial power, while civil war in the Sudan, and military dictatorship in Ghana and Nigeria emerged following their granting of independence by the United Kingdom government.

Since independence Zambia has held a democratic election in which President Kaunda was defeated. Malawi continued to be ruled in a dictatorial manner until the very recent death of President Banda. Zimbabwe did have a little publicized tribal dispute shortly after becoming independent when the majority Shona government under Mugabe eliminated a large number of Sendebele tribesmen in Matabeleland, but the Sendebele leader Joshua Nkomo is now a Cabinet minister in the Mugabe government. In comparison with other African states, post-independence violence in the Central African territories has been insignificant and long may it endure.

Readers of this autobiography might have gained the impression that we were pro-African and anti-European in our outlook. I strongly deny that this was the case, for we never joined any political party or took an active part in any pro-African organization in Central Africa. The explanation is that we were conscious of natural justice, and in describing events as we observed and participated in them it became abundantly clear to us that most European governments and some Europeans treated the concept of natural justice with contempt.

As I commenced this unscholarly treatise with two examples of race relations, I now bring it to an end with a further case in point. When I was medical superintendent of the large African infectious diseases hospital in Salisbury, now Harare, the matron, who was a deeply religious male registered nurse, often called my attention to the fact that all the trained medical orderlies employed in the hospital, about 30 in number, were Christians, with the exception of one who preferred to remain a heathen. As this appeared to worry the matron, without any serious intent I approached the odd man out and asked him outright why he did not convert to Christianity. He replied that there was no difference between Christianity and his own beliefs. I then pointed out that I was aware that as a non-Christian he believed in Madzimu (an omniscient god acceptable to most religious beliefs) and that his main credence was to worship his ancestral spirits and not to recognize Christ the Son of God. He then asked me if I would kindly accompany him to the second floor of the hospital where one side of a ward overlooked the Harare European cemetery. He pointed out the large number of mourners attending to or planting flowers on graves. Others stood meditating, or perhaps even praying, alongside the graves of their departed loved ones. I was asked the inevitable question, 'Is this not an example of family spirit worship? So you see, Sir! What is the difference?' My *sotto voce* reply merely repeated the question, 'Yes! What is the difference?'

Finally I have to explain the significance of the use of the singular 'I' in some situations, while in others the plural 'we' is employed. This refers to my beloved wife who died before the writing of this book was completed. We had over 50 years of married bliss together in which we shared all our pleasures with the occasional displeasure. Without her encouragement, help and assistance it would not have been possible for me to have pursued a rewarding professional career under difficult circumstances in an unstable part of the world. I dedicate this book to her memory!

Index